# Culturally Competent Engagement: A Mindful Approach

# BOOK ENDORSEMENTS

*Culturally Competent Engagement: A Mindful Approach* engages the reader with carefully developed exercises and activities that encourage reflection and personal growth. These activities help the reader live more consciously and compassionately in a diverse and changing world. Being culturally competent is critical to addressing the challenges of today and this book succeeds in helping us realize that ability.

—John P Miller
*Professor at the University of Toronto, Canada*
*and author of The Holistic Curriculum*

This is a highly valuable book. The book provides thoughtful contemplative practices that educators can employ to equip learners with skills to gain a greater awareness of themselves, a deep, appreciative understanding of others, and a critical perspective on power and privileges in the systems of inequality in our world. The book is a must read for transformative educators who aspire to facilitate learners' effective development of cultural engagement competencies embedded in respect, humility, appreciation, empathy, and inclusiveness.

—Jing Lin
*Harold R. W. Benjamin Professor of International Education*
*University of Maryland, USA*

This book features a number of stimulating self-reflective and contemplative classroom activities for diversity-minded instructors to foster learning through mindfulness and peer engagement. The authors draw on multiple cultural traditions, symbol interpretation, and self-deprecating examples of cross-cultural insight and humility that help center the reader's thinking about new ways of using facets of their authentic selves in the classroom. Instructors looking to broaden their toolkit to consider the educational benefits of relationship-building and self-disclosure can learn many practical techniques to enhance the classroom environment.

—Matt Lee
*Teaching Professor of Human Services*
*Northeastern University, USA*

# Culturally Competent
# Engagement: A Mindful Approach

Edward J. Brantmeier
Noorie K. Brantmeier

INFORMATION AGE PUBLISHING, INC.
Charlotte, NC • www.infoagepub.com

**Library of Congress Cataloging-In-Publication Data**

The CIP data for this book can be found on the Library of Congress website (loc.gov).

Paperback: 978-1-64802-174-9
Hardcover: 978-1-64802-175-6
E-Book: 978-1-64802-176-3

# CONTENTS

# ACKNOWLEDGEMENTS

We thank the following people for contributing ideas, quotes, and input on this book: Imane Zirari; Lauren Jefferson; Jared Featherstone; Sarah Featherstone; Cathryn Molloy; Manoj Mishra; David Levy; John. P. Miller; Matthew Ezzell; Jing Lin; Becca Howes-Mischel; Matt Lee; Tanya Laffler; Zachary Williams; Andrew Strack; Media Production Services; JMU Libraries; Mark Meredith; and Tyree Chavious. Special thanks to Seven Sisters Community Development Group, LLC.

We especially want to thank James Madison University, the College of Education, and the Center for Faculty Innovation at James Madison University. With mission and vision resonance, we hope to add to commiserate efforts toward creating engaged, enlightened, and culturally competent global citizens.

We wrote this book prior to the COVID-19 pandemic of Spring, 2020 and recognize and align with the significant momentum of the Black Lives Matter Movement. We see this book as one small tool, among many, that can be used for racial justice and equity.

# DEDICATION

We dedicate this book to our children and to all who locate themselves in multiple cultural worlds.

# PREFACE

We live in a world filled with much misunderstanding. Living with awareness, compassion, and humility can change misunderstanding into opportunities to learn and grow. The writing of this book comes from a place of experiential learning, reflection, and hope. We are hopeful that with deliberate and intentional study of self, others, and systems, people can learn to deeply connect with "others" and also appreciate difference and actively embrace diversity as a life-affirming opportunity. We chose to write this book to create a little more peace through connection in an all-too-often violent, divisive world. Our motivation has been to share what we have learned and taught to a much wider public audience—beyond the walls of our classrooms and consulting meeting rooms. Our inspiration is to create a better future for our multi-racial and multicultural children and family.

The process of writing this book involved struggle, challenge, joy, and insight. We have been thinking about and discussing the contents of this book in formal meetings, lunch dates, dinner dates, reflections on teaching in the evenings before bed, and in our many family and solo travel adventures over the last 20 years together. The idea to write a book on cultural competence emerged about fifteen years ago. In making ideas a reality, we spent two and a half years, from proposal to final draft, to complete this book project. We sought guidance from colleagues, friends, editors, and graduate students in the process.

It is not exactly easy to write with a balance of head and heart to an unknown audience of the future. We struggled with how much to share regarding our personal journeys, what the purpose of this book is, who the audience is, and our own

*Culturally Competent Engagement: A Mindful Approach,* pages xi–xii.
Copyright © 2020 by Information Age Publishing
All rights of reproduction in any form reserved.

sense of not knowing everything about the topic. Yet we believe that the process of writing an article, a book, whatever, is one of exploration—combining what others know with what we know, in an effort to advance the horizon of knowing through experience. Writing from a place of personal and professional experience is empowering because we come to know ourselves, our strengths, limitations, and motivations. In coming to know ourselves, we open the possibility of knowing others in a more substantive way. Connecting with diverse others is an essential skill, necessary for survival and for thriving.

*—Eddie and Noorie Brantmeier*
*Shenandoah Valley, Virginia, U.S.A.*
*January, 2020*

CHAPTER 1

# INTRODUCTION TO THE SELF, OTHER, SYSTEMS APPROACH

In an increasingly diverse and globally interconnected world, being culturally competent in our personal, professional, and civic lives is more relevant than ever. Being globally connected requires a high degree of awareness and skill in order to smoothly navigate complex contexts, situations, and relationships. In a linguistically rich and culturally diverse world, the confluence of people and cultures requires habits of mind, dispositions, skills, and values that promote diversity affirmation while simultaneously honoring one's own cultural integrity and limitations. The benefits of being culturally competent are numerous and include healthy, holistic relationships and connection with people across differences.

An education for intercultural competence that fosters awareness and connection helps to positively embrace diversity, promote equity, and foster inclusion in our work, social, and civic life. Bennett (2008 ) defines intercultural competence as "a set of cognitive, affective, and behavioral skills and characteristics that support effective and appropriate interaction in a variety of cultural contexts" (p. 122). Cultivating thought patterns, socio-emotional capacities, culturally congruent behaviors, and the adaptive intelligence required for positive and meaningful interactions with others requires commitment to a process of lifelong learning, inside, and outside the classroom walls. A task force of the Association of American Colleges and Universities (2009) provides some guidance about why this work matters:

*Culturally Competent Engagement: A Mindful Approach,* pages 1–19.
Copyright © 2020 by Information Age Publishing

The call to integrate intercultural knowledge and competence into the heart of education is an imperative born of seeing ourselves as members of a world community, knowing that we share the future with others. Beyond mere exposure to culturally different others, the campus community requires the capacity to: meaningfully engage those others, place social justice in historical and political context, and put culture at the core of transformative learning (p. 1).

One path to becoming more aware of ourselves as cultural beings, learning more deeply about others, and considering the ways larger systems impact diverse groups is through a mindful approach. Mindfulness and contemplative movements in higher education aim to create a more just and compassionate society (Center for Contemplative Mind and Society, n.d.-a). The global contemplative movement in higher education, co-led by the Association of Contemplative Mind and Society in the United States, aims to facilitate a deeper way of learning and knowing for deeper connection and inclusion, an effort that we align with by writing this book. Culturally competent and contemplative people are needed for the compassionate work toward equity and equality.

Mindfulness involves focus, attention, observation, and insight, "Mindfulness means maintaining a moment-by-moment awareness of our thoughts, feelings, bodily sensations, and surrounding environment, through a gentle, nurturing lens" (Greater Good Magazine, n.d.). Simply stated, **mindful cultural engagement** is an attitude and approach of self-awareness of one's thoughts, feelings, bodily sensations and an awareness of oneself as a cultural being. We are all people comprised of accumulated influences from many sources, including family, community, and more. Mindful cultural engagement involves, on a moment-to-moment basis, monitoring one's own mind, emotions, and body, without judgement. It also involves critical self-reflection about how cultural conditioning influences thought, emotion, bodily reaction, and action. If we understand culture as Spradley (1997) defines it, "…the learned, shared knowledge that people use to generate behavior and interpret experience," (p. 18), then mindful cultural engagement is observing that acquired knowledge in an objective way to fully understand the source of thought patterns, emotions, and behaviors. In understanding the sources of thought patterns, emotions, and behaviors we can affirm or examine them to more fully understanding who we are as cultural beings. This self-awareness can potentially lead to changes in interpretation and behavior; it invites fresh possibilities for growth and self-actualization.

In addition to self-awareness, mindful cultural engagement involves being open to difference and available to receive and understand it. Without clinging or grasping to one's assumptions, meanings, interpretations, or habits of mind, mindful cultural engagement involves being open to fully experiencing the other in the present moment. Mindful cultural engagement requires deeply understanding one's own conditioning and context while appreciating the conditioning and context of others. This approach assumes a holistic interpretation of experiences and associated meanings in diverse settings; it requires sensitivity to details and to one's total relational experience.

We, thus, consider the approach taken in this book a "mindful" approach to culturally competent engagement: mindful of a long-term and ongoing process; mindful of the moment; mindful of judgment; mindful of multiple courses of action; and mindful of one's own limitations. We use mindfulness (lowercase m) in an everyday sense in regards to observing one's experience and "focusing attention," yet we also use Mindfulness (uppercase M) in relation to honoring diversity and interdependence. Mindfulness is a tool for this, and you, students, educators, and citizens, are needed in the effort. When we explore the concept of mindfulness, we can think of a continuum, as shown in Table 1.1 below:

Non-judgmental awareness is paying attention to the present moment in daily experience. Metacognition is observing the mind to understand patterned ways of thinking, emotional reactions, and physical sensations of the body. Awareness of interdependence is simply when one observes connection and calmly abides in experiences—positive, negative, or neutral; in this mindful state we acknowledge the deep diversity of human experience and honor a fundamental ground of unity in relationship to one another.

Hours of contemplation and seclusion are not required for mindful, culturally competent engagement. In fact, as the authors of this book, we have very different approaches and meanings related to mindfulness and contemplative practice. Eddie has been a contemplative practitioner, using a variety of disciplined meditations, nature immersion, and martial arts exercises for over 25 years. Noorie has been a Native American powwow dancer and has enjoyed photography and drawing for decades, yet is a newcomer to mindfulness meditation. We celebrate and invite a diversity of contemplative ways of centering, knowing, and learning, and point to the tree of contemplative practices to illustrate a diversity of practices (Center for Contemplative Mind and Society, n.d.-b). Daily non-judgmental awareness, metacognition, and recognition of the paradox of unity in diversity are all part of building mindful cultural competence—one experience at a time, one moment at a time.

Why walk the life-long path of culturally competent engagement in a contemplative way? Barbezat and Bush (2014) maintain that "...contemplative methods are powerful means for a deeper engagement with life and greater insight into ourselves and others" (p. 38). Culturally competent engagement is about lifelong learning, for the purpose of deeper connection and the cultivation of quality relationships with those who are culturally different from you. Seeing difference as

TABLE 1.1.  Mindfulness Continuum

| Non-Judgement | Metacognition | Interdependence |
| --- | --- | --- |
| Observing the present moment | Observing mind, patterned thinking | Observing diversity, connection, and unity |

an asset rather than a deficit affords us opportunities for positive relationships and the potential for social change. For those of us in helping professions or positions where we work with historically marginalized individuals and groups of people, we can more effectively help others from a place of authentic and empathetic understanding about their lived realities. We can more deeply see the why of certain conditions, behaviors, or responses and more compassionately provide viable proactive solutions to the complex challenges people face on a day-to-day basis.

In addition to effectively helping others, it is also enjoyable to learn about what other people do, feel, value, and habitually think. Learning about oneself and others can be a fascinating journey, fueled by curiosity, and peppered with meaningful insight. For example, recall a moment when you took pause to grasp, truly grasp, a position on an issue (for example, climate change, religious conviction, gun laws, or sexual attraction) that was profoundly different from your own. Did deeply understanding the perspective enrich your own life? Did this new lens on the world instill an appreciation of difference? The vast differences in human cultural diversity provide needed variety, which some consider to be the savory spices of life. Cultural differences are not to be changed, assimilated, absorbed; they are to be deeply understood and celebrated as part of the tapestry of human experience. Culturally competent engagement, as a lifelong path or journey, can be an ongoing discovery of the vast diversity of human cognition, behavior, emotions, and ways of knowing.

## OUR APPROACH IN THIS BOOK

We intend for this book to be practical and easily put to use. We hope readers will utilize this book to generate levels of self-awareness, strengthen the skills for exploring their own assumptions and implicit biases, and learn new paths for connecting with others (i.e., empathy, perspective taking, critical thinking). Typical approaches to developing cultural competence focus on acquisition of communicative skills, behaviors, and dispositions needed to effectively navigate cross-cultural relationships and function effectively in multicultural environments. (Association of American Colleges and Universities, 2009; Bennett, 1993; Diller & Moule, 2005) We include and build on this typical approach of self-awareness and skills to understand others by adding a layer of critical and complex systems understanding as a necessary foundation for effective cross-cultural engagement.

When engaging with others in culturally competent ways, we hope that individuals will forge authentic connections with others while being mindful to not minimize differences into uniformity or sameness, because; multicultural difference is a strength. This book arises from that core belief. Therefore, we hope to provide tools in this book that will help you mindfully and compassionately engage with realities and possibilities when you encounter and navigate difference, so that you may be more conscious of who you are and how you can build bridges of connection with others. Our intention is to share insights, tools, and experiences that will generate more self-awareness and positive interactions, so that you may have deepened connection and relationship with others from various cultures and backgrounds. Similarly, it is important for you, the reader, to clarify your intentions for investing your valuable time by reading this book. What brought you to this moment in your life? Why are you reading this? What intentions do you have for your own growth and learning? What do you hope to learn, challenge, or overcome by reading this book?

## STRUCTURE OF THE BOOK

Chapters in this book are arranged in accordance with the Self-Other-Systems (S.O.S.) Approach and will include theory, research, examples, and learning exercises to promote capacities for cultural competence (Brantmeier & Brantmeier, 2015). We incorporate learning exercises in order to promote direct experience with the discussed techniques and in order to foster ongoing reflection. The S.O.S approach is a three-step method where readers will be asked in separate chapter of the book to examine themselves, consider tools for connecting with others, and then examine systemic influences. The learning exercise are evidence-demonstrated, meaning that they have been tried and proven effective in learning environments in the United States and elsewhere. When used for teaching and learning cultural competence, the S.O.S. Approach has helped students and business clients grow and demonstrate mindful and sensitive learning and engagement. In essence, this book reflects our past and present practice and emergent ideas on a complex topic.

We chose simple acronyms, S.O.S. (Self-Other-Systems) to organize the book and to aid memory; readers can, thus, quickly use these techniques on the go and in the moment. Chapter One, this chapter, serves as the introduction to the book and provides and overview of the self-other-systems approach. It provides key terms and definitions for clarity and for foundational knowledge. Cross cultural snapshots are provided to provide readers insight into the authors and their unique experiences of multicultural environments. Chapter Two focuses on self- understanding and provides three powerful learning experiences aimed at promoting awareness of oneself as a cultural being. Chapter Three provides a theoretical and experiential exploration for appreciating and learning about cultural differences and similarities. Chapter Four focuses on examining societal structures through theory and practice that involve critical and complex systems thinking; arguably, the content of chapter four is the most difficult material of the book. Finally, Chapter Five explores the integration of self, other, and systems understanding and reiterates that learning about oneself, others, and systems is a lifelong journey. We seek to offer an integrated approach that honors the aims and purposes of holistic education, which are centered in connection (Miller, 2008).

If we are honest with ourselves, we openly admit we never really know the whole story about others, and rarely do we even understand our own story. Yet, with an attitude of humility and a deep respect for the unknown, we move forward in search of finding out where our story lines converge and diverge in rather different directions. Yet the stories that are our lives have depth and nuance and can be influenced by the smallest of incidents and insights. For instance, a certain teacher or opportunity, presented at the right time in our lives—whether by chance, serendipity, or random coincidence—can make us pause, change course or remain steady on the path. In truth, we cannot teach the golden recipes for culturally competent engagement. We can only provide tools for the path. In what follows this introduction chapter, we offer a brief biography of the authors and then two moments in time for readers to more deeply understand the challenges of multicultural encounters. After that, we offer a more in-depth explanation of the S.O.S. approach, key terms and definitions, and a learning exercise to close this chapter.

## WHO ARE THE AUTHORS?

This book is simultaneously personal and professional, drawing on our own unique experiences and over forty years of combined experience working in higher education, communities, and businesses with diverse people. Together, we (Noorie and Eddie) live in a multicultural, multi-ethnic home with our multicultural and multi-ethnic/racial children. We travel in and out of different cultural worlds when we visit family, neighbors, friends, and for our work in the United States and around the world. We have lived, taught, studied and worked in diverse contexts, including the Netherlands, India, Cyprus, Australia, Nicaragua, Fiji, St. Louis, Navajo Nation, northern Colorado, Austria, and Thailand, which required a great deal of cultural competence. As university professors, we have taught courses that integrate learning exercises for culturally competent engagement, and have witnessed tremendous growth in our students who intentionally and deeply engage with the material and methods that we seek to share in this book. Yet, we both have our own unique lenses from which we interpret the world and we seek to share that diversity, too.

Noorie is an Indigenous/Latina/Black cisgender person who has taught research methods, consulting, diversity, and Indigenous Studies courses at several major U.S. universities. She has lived, worked, and explored diverse U.S. domestic and international contexts as an AmeriCorps volunteer, educator, social worker, research consultant, and entrepreneur. She is a third culture kid who spent six of her formative childhood years attending a highly multicultural, international school while living in the Netherlands with her family. She is a founding partner of Seven Sisters Community Development Group, LLC, a business whose mission is to offer culturally relevant and innovative strategies, services, and products that create systemic change in low-wealth and diverse communities across the United States (see http://www.7sistersconsulting.com). As a consultant, she has more than a decade of experience helping build cultural bridges between Native American communities and diverse stakeholders through community-based research and evaluation efforts, as well as culturally-matched curriculum development for tribal communities. Noorie has led university students on semester abroad programs in Spain and has co-presented research with her students in Portugal and Scotland—serving as an example for culturally competent engagement.

Eddie is a white, cisgender, heterosexual male, who comes from a low socio-economic status background. He grew up in rural Wisconsin and has farming roots. His early, rare experiences with diverse others fueled a passion of learning more about difference. He is a first-generation college student and has taught cross-cultural education, multicultural education, and foundations of education courses at the university level for over fifteen years. Eddie has been both a K–12 and university educator, and diversity consultant working in culturally and linguistically diverse environments in the United States and around the world. He has lived and worked in India, Nepal, Thailand, the Philippines, Cyprus, the Navajo Nation in the United States, among other places and has expertise in engaging university students in community service learning, domestically and internationally. Eddie has been a contemplative practitioner for over 25 years, mainly grounding his practice in mindfulness traditions, martial arts, and nature immersion. Eddie was a Fulbright Scholar in India in 2009 and has given research talks in Brazil, Nepal, India, Austria, Germany, the United States, and England.

Together, we raise three boys who walk in and out of the multiple cultural worlds of our extended family. We currently live in the agrarian Shenandoah Valley of Virginia, in proximity to Washington, D.C. and other urban centers. We seek to encourage cultural competence so that, together, we can build bridges, forge connections, and create more justice and peace in a world where misunderstandings and misconceptions have the potential to lead to subtle forms of bias or violence, especially when they are often rooted in broader cultural and structural violence. In essence, the focus of this book—creating culturally competent people and citizens—emerges from our lived experience and hope for our children.

## CROSS-CULTURAL SNAPSHOT: NOORIE

Prior to flying to California from Virginia, my business partner and I designed and developed a one-day training workshop on building cultural bridges for housing counselors that we would be co-facilitating. Housing counselors are approved by the U.S. Department of Housing and Urban Development and are tasked with providing guidance and support for homeowners in danger of losing their homes or having difficulty paying their mortgages. The day before the workshop, I flew from Virginia to Sacramento, California and arrived at Sacramento International

Airport around 9:00 pm. It had been a long day traveling from the east to the west coast, and whenever I land in an unfamiliar city, which is fairly often as a consultant, my first needs are to get to my hotel quickly and then find food. Instead of taking a taxi, I pulled up my Uber app and thankfully, a driver arrived quickly. As we drove toward the hotel, I watched the map on my Uber app and began to take in my surroundings. The closer we got to the hotel, all of the businesses, churches, social service agencies, and advertising were all in Korean. A long stretch of building was filled with graffiti and I saw a group of teens with hooded sweatshirts walking and conversing with one another. Everyone I saw on the streets was Asian and I was embarrassed that I could not be more specific about the country of origin. The Uber driver let me out and said, "This isn't a great part of town. I especially don't recommend walking around here at night." He pointed to a street off in the distance and tells me not to go beyond a certain point for my own safety. When I entered the Hampton Inn, I realized I was the only non-Korean person in the lobby. I was quickly checked in by a Korean receptionist and received my hotel keys. After a tiring day, I finally made it to my room and looked forward to ordering room service. I opened the menu, which was in Korean, with only short explanations in English, and all of the foods on the menu were in Korean or Chinese. I made a selection that sounded delicious and called down to order room service about 10 minutes before the hotel restaurant was due to close. The person I connected with told me in broken English that they are closed for the evening. At this point, I was tired, disappointed, hungry, and had resigned myself to eating a granola bar for dinner. Heading into the shower, I noticed the signage in the bathroom was in Korean. My guess was that the sign was about water temperature, but I wasn't entirely sure. Finally, I sunk into bed and took stock of my situation. I was hungry, concerned about my safety, and baffled by my sense that I had left the United States when I knew for a fact that I was in California.

As an avid traveler, I have felt this sense of unease and discomfort before when travelling abroad. I also recognized that my thought patterns had turned somewhat negative as I tried to settle down for the night. My thoughts drifted to Asian gangs and I considered my safety in this area of the city and the graffiti I saw; I wondered why room service closed early and did not accommodate my request; and I wondered why I was on this thought train when I would be facilitating conversations on issues of diversity the next day. As a multiracial Native American/Black/Puerto-Rican woman, third-culture kid, and college professor who teaches cultural diversity courses, I am not free from having unconscious biases. The primary agents of socialization—family, school, peers, and the mass media—impact me in ways that have to be "checked." While watching television with my parents as a teenager in the mid-1990s, I remember the media often representing Asian American youth as "gangbangers." What the media does not mention is that some Asian American youth in the 1990s actively rebelled against the model minority stereotype, but were also looking for acceptance and connection in an often unaccepting society. Checking myself means asking where my association with young, Asian American males and gangs stem from, and how valid is it? The truth is we all have unconscious bias, and as evidenced from my own example, people of color are also guilty of internalizing messages and images from our families, peers, schools, and the media. From inappropriate or racist jokes told in a family setting, to the histories and voices we hear or do not hear in our K–12 schools, the kids who are included or excluded in our peer groups, and the myths perpetuated in the media about women and/or people who are deemed a threat to the American way of life, we are all influenced by agents of socialization. With that lens and from a place of acceptance, we must consider mindfulness as an approach to reflect on and check our own biases before they become action.

After reflecting on my initial experiences in Sacramento and the disorientation I felt, I was able to adjust to my new setting. Being able to adjust quickly in a new cultural context becomes easier with time and repeated exposure. One approach to adjusting and better understanding a new cultural context is the Observe, Infer, Inquire, Respond (OIIR) method, which we will discuss in more detail later in the book and will provide practical examples of the method in action.

## CROSS-CULTURAL SNAPSHOT: EDDIE

I entered a pit-style lecture hall in Varanasi, India. Wooden chairs, filling the rows of each terrace, were occupied by eager students staring down at me. Sunil, a young male Hindu student, stood up, placed his hands together over the middle of his chest, bowed, and proceeded to bend down reverently toward the ground so that he could touch my feet. He touched my feet and then his own head. It was a gesture of high honor; I was his teacher, and he was showing a level of respect for the teacher-student relationship that dates back thousands of years in Indian cultural tradition. *Matha, Pitha, Guru, Deviam*—the Sanskrit phrase that translates to English as: mother, father, teacher, God—is often quoted in Hinduism. Its meaning is at once subtle and powerful: the first teacher is the mother, then the father, then a guru who teaches spiritual texts and subtleties, and, finally, God with whom one has the potential to cultivate direct realization. As a male, Hindu student at Banaras Hindu University, Sunil conveyed reverence for the student-teacher relationship by bowing and touching my feet—an act of supplication and honor. At first, it surely made me very uncomfortable.

As a professor from the United States and as a Fulbright scholar representing my country, I wanted my students to view me as an equal, as a co-learner, and as a guide for their learning processes. In fact, based on my own cultural conditioning and personal leanings toward power equilibrium in relationships, I wanted to stop him from bowing to touch my feet when I entered the classroom. Over the course of our time together, I folded my hands, bowed, and reciprocated namaste with Sunil. I became comfortable with this part of our greeting ritual. Yet when he touched my feet, I remained uneasy. This awkwardness, of course, is a classic example of cross-cultural conflict where gestures, meanings, thought patterns, and values clash; both Sunil and I had very different interpretations and comfort levels with these interactions.

In the lifelong learning journey of culturally competent engagement, I gained a deeper level of self-understanding from this particular interactive scene. Sunil bowing to me, his teacher, was not really about me; it was about what I represented to Sunil. Touching a teacher's feet is an act that honors a sacred lineage and the continuity of knowledge transmitted through the precious relationship of learning between a teacher and student, or guru and disciple. In Varanasi, India, as a Fulbright-Nehru scholar lecturing on multicultural dynamics in peace education efforts, I was very far from my familiar cultural context—a university classroom in the United States. If I was going to adapt and thrive in this context, I needed to observe, interpret, and respond skillfully to a myriad of cross-cultural encounters of daily life at the intellectually and culturally vibrant Banaras Hindu University (See Figure 1.1: Cultural Conflict).

I had taken Sunil's touching my feet as a personal thing, and it was not at all personal. In order to come to this realization, I asked myself: "Why did this feel uncomfortable? Why did I feel so uneasy?" I observed my emotional reactions when reflecting on the incident later. I simultaneously felt honored and uneasy

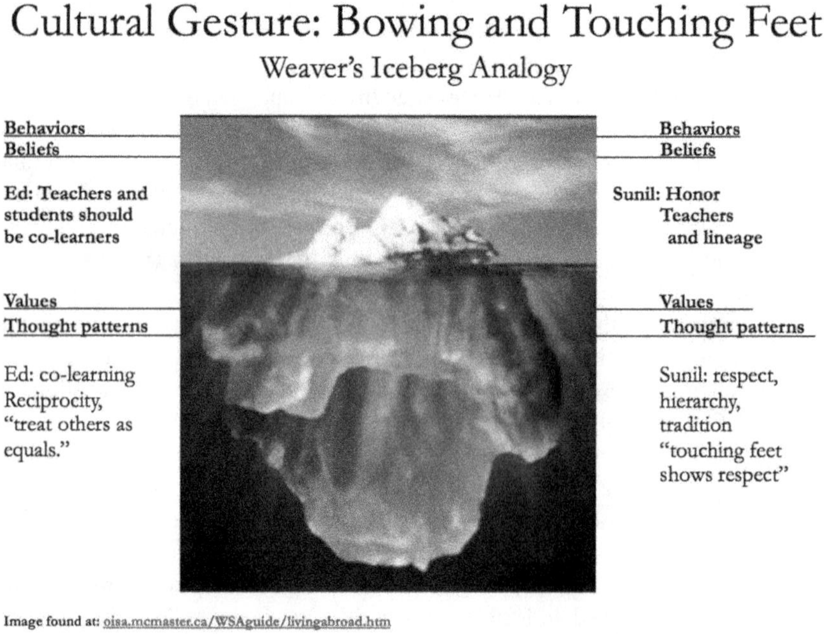

## Cultural Gesture: Bowing and Touching Feet
### Weaver's Iceberg Analogy

| Behaviors | Behaviors |
| Beliefs | Beliefs |

Ed: Teachers and students should be co-learners

Sunil: Honor Teachers and lineage

| Values | Values |
| Thought patterns | Thought patterns |

Ed: co-learning Reciprocity, "treat others as equals."

Sunil: respect, hierarchy, tradition "touching feet shows respect"

Image found at: oisa.mcmaster.ca/WSAguide/livingabroad.htm

FIGURE 1.1.   Cultural Conflict

with an act that I interpreted as submissive and compliant. I observed the behavior, I made inferences about what the behavior actually meant, and then as time passed, I checked with my Indian colleague and friend Manoj who simply conveyed he was displaying a more traditional form of respect—bowing and touching the feet of one's esteemed teacher. Indian society, much like the United States, is highly stratified with various hierarchies and roles in play during daily interactions. People perform various cultural roles that are highly dependent on circumstance and context. I became comfortable with our brief interchanges when I entered the classroom. We would mutually bow, he would touch my feet, and we would get on with class. It became, for lack of a better word, normal.

Yet one morning, I felt particularly playful. When Sunil bowed down to touch my feet, I smiled and reciprocated, bowing down to touch Sunil's feet. But he quickly jerked away from me. He was insulted, and I could tell I had made a huge cross-cultural mistake. What I did not realize in my playful response was that I was breaking a longstanding tradition of thousands of years. I was playing with a reverence for the teacher-student role set. I wanted to convey that we indeed are equal co-learners on the path to mutual discovery in the classroom. And yet I insulted Sunil by my lighthearted gesture and, honestly, our relationship was never quite the same.

After this incident, Sunil continued to bow and touch my feet, yet I could tell he was now uneasy with the exchange and a bit fearful that I would reciprocate by touching his feet again. What I learned is that our assumptions, our gestures, our mistakes, and our own vulnerability in cross-cultural interactions often end up being our best teachers. Mistakes are inevitable; what matters is how and what we learn from them.

As our opening snapshots make clear, we are not born with cultural competence; rather, it is cultivated through repeated exposure to difference and through a commitment to practice in the spirit of learning and growth. Culturally competent engagement requires a great deal of humility, vulnerability, reflection, learning, and growth. While an open mind truly helps on this path, there is also a willingness to stretch and massage one's comfort zone. Recognition and validation of deep difference helps to move beyond one's self understanding and limitations. True culturally competent engagement involves making mistakes and learning from them. Over time, performing everyday acts of engaging with others, observing their effects, reflecting on the outcomes, and modifying assumptions, expectations, communication, and behavior accordingly, becomes second nature.

## THE SELF, OTHER, SYSTEMS APPROACH

Globalization, immigration, and the fact that the fastest growing racial group in the United States, the authors' home country, is multi-ethnic/racial people provide a situational context where the cultivation of cultural competence is vitally im-

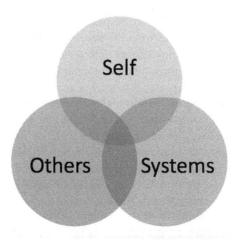

FIGURE 1.2.   Self, Others, and Systems Model

portant. Given multi-ethnic, multicultural realities in the United States and else-where, citizens will require inclusive values, mindsets, and high degrees of skill to effectively navigate 21st Century life.

The S.O.S. approach (Brantmeier & Brantmeier, 2015) is a model that aligns with and builds on the existing approaches to cultural competence development by including a critical component: examining and critiquing the systems of pow-er, oppression, and privilege that influence and affect the lives of individuals and groups of people (See Figure 1.2: Self, Others, and Systems Model).

Self-understanding requires the cultivation of mindful, moment-to-moment awareness and an ability to choose from a range of possible actions. For example, through mindfulness practice, you can create an observation of bias in thought when perceiving the behavior of a cultural other. When bias is recognized, you can choose to react negatively, positively, or neutrally. In addition to recognition of bias, reflective engagement is essential in order to fully experience and thrive in all that multicultural environments have to offer. Other understanding is culti-vated by developing the habits and skills that allow you to be open to difference, to fully receive the other, and to more fully understand their values, beliefs, and behaviors. It is our strong position that all of these dispositions, skills, and habits can be learned through practice. We assume that habits of mind, behaviors, and values can be nurtured, taught, and learned over time in a process of creating vibrant, multicultural home environments, communities, and societies. That said, no one is really an expert at culturally competent engagement, since as co-learn-ing in cross-cultural encounters can be an opportunity for self-awareness, connec-tion to others, and collective change. We are always in the process of becoming culturally competent; it is something we must engage with for life.

## KEY DEFINITIONS AND TERMS

**Cultural competence**, as we explore it in the Self, Other, and Systems approach in this book, involves self-awareness and challenging one's own assumptions in the process. Cultural competence also involves skills for interpreting cultural others, which includes intercultural empathy and a deep appreciation of the diversity of otherness. People who embody cultural competence demonstrate "openness towards other cultures, respect for different values and curiosity, knowledge of the self and the other, and awareness of cultural difference" (Krajewski, 2011, p. 138). In addition to the personal and interpersonal, our conception of cultural competence in this book involves an awareness of how to navigate cultural, political, economic, social, and environmental systems that enable or constrain access, hope, dreams, and happiness. Thus, our approach involves developing our own self-awareness, the skills to engage the other, and a complex awareness of how systems circumscribe and influence daily life.

The term **culturally competent engagement**, as used in this book, refers to a dynamic, ongoing, and fluid process of knowing oneself and others—of being fully open and present, in the moment, to *how* you are observing and receptive to others. *What* is arising and happening for others in your interactions? Culturally competent engagement is a process, not a fixed goal; it is not a finish line that you cross one day and the race is suddenly over. In fact, it is not a race at all; it is a lifelong journey. The danger of using terms like culturally competent engagement is that they may suggest that there is an end goal or that it is a game—cultural competence is achieved and then "poof," you are done. You have arrived; you are now competent. We recognize that competence is a tricky term, given that it implies, "The ability to do something successfully or efficiently" (Lexico, n.d.). Rather than precise application of a method or effectiveness, we perceive culturally competent engagement as a constant process that requires adaptive intelligence and ongoing learning—but you can get better at it with time and practice. Cushner, McClelland, and Safford (2003) maintain, "Intercultural competence is not achieved in one course or one experience. Rather, you recognize where one is on the developmental continuum, and you engage in systematic, oftentimes repetitious, and well-planned exposure to intercultural interactions that are designed to nudge you to increasingly complex levels" (p. 130). Moving toward increasingly complex levels of knowing, being, and doing is our intention in this book. Loving the process of learning about oneself and others in our dynamic world is another intention.

Terms like **intercultural**, **multicultural**, and **cross-cultural** can be confusing and may be used interchangeably in this book. "**Multi**" roughly means many; "**inter**" means between; and "**cross**" also can mean between. We assume that encounters with individuals and communities that are different from your "usual" are multicultural in a modern world; rarely do we interact with just one cultural "other" at a time. In addition, individuals are often multicultural, meaning they are comprised of multiple cultural influences and have learned to perform different cultural role sets in different contexts. Identity is often multiple, contextual, and fluid (Banks et al., 2005). In this sense, an open approach that assumes complexity when engaging with others in a multicultural world seems like a reasonable one.

The debate regarding a definition of **culture** in cultural anthropology runs deep with theory and nuance. Yet we will spare you that ongoing conversation here by providing a useable, everyday definition of culture "…the learned, shared knowledge that people use to generate behavior and interpret experience," (Spradley, 1997, p. 18). People acquire culture through learning; as a child or as an adult, we learn from those around us, often in group settings. With this acquired knowledge, we interpret our own experiences, while making sense of the experience of others. We also generate acceptable behaviors for a given context. Specific behaviors hold vastly different meanings for people across contexts. For example, a smile in the United States often conveys friendliness or happiness, yet it can be perceived as a negative, interpersonal boundary crossing or intimate advance in other cultural contexts. Being able to understand subtle perceptions and meanings in diverse contexts is an acquired skill in culturally competent engagement. Being aware of our own socialization, and the perceptions and meanings of others, frees us so that we can choose to act in responsive, life-giving ways. Being a good human being who exhibits empathy, compassion, acceptance, patience, forgiveness, and generosity can be something that is beyond culture—though recognizing ways of expressing empathy, compassion, and generosity is surely culturally situated and contextual.

## LEARNING EXERCISE ONE: CONCEPT MAPPING USING THE S.O.S. APPROACH

*Overview*

For many, conceptual frameworks are challenging to understand unless connected with a practical application. To make the S.O.S. framework come to life, concept mapping can help you see the connections between and among variables, while providing an opportunity to consider your own social identities and the experiences of others.

## LEARNING EXERCISE

Learners will make progress toward:

- Situating the S.O.S. model in holistic context;
- Visually representing concepts and relating them to your personal lives; and

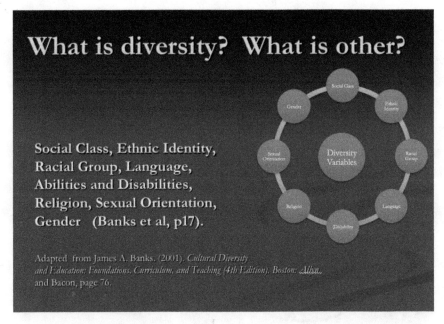

FIGURE 1.3.  Diversity Variables

• Discerning areas for continued growth and learning.

*Instructions*

Concept mapping works best on a large-scale using tools such as flipcharts and markers or white boards. Seeing the concepts visually can help you make new connections and possibly consider multiple perspectives. Introducing participants, as an instructor, to the diversity wheel and discussing multiple diversity variables can be an effective way to help people consider their own intersecting identities (See Figure 1.3: Diversity Variables).

Using the Venn diagram as a guide, ask yourself the following questions:

Self:  What are my social identities? (Female, middle class, multiracial, etc.)

Others:  What are the identities of individuals and groups who are different than I am? Which groups do I have less experience interacting with? To increase my personal cultural competence, which groups do I need to learn about and from?

Systems:  What societal structures influence or impact my life and/or the lives of others? Where have I learned about and interacted with people culturally different than myself?

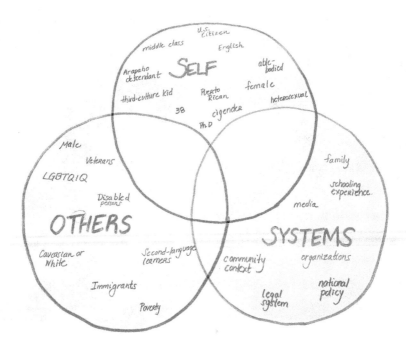

FIGURE 1.4. Noorie's Self, Other, System Diagram

Figure 1.4 is provided as an example to begin mapping the social identities that shape our own worldview, considering examples of cultural others, and brainstorming larger societal structures and systems that influence our experiences.

After spending quality time thinking and writing your ideas in the Self, Other, and Systems circles, look at the center of your diagram where the three come together. We suggest using a Venn Diagram because they allow us to examine differences, but also where ideas come together for form a whole. The empty space, the place where all three come together—the self, the other, and the systems that influence and circumscribe our lives comprises the core of cultural competence—awareness of all three areas. Gaze on the place of convergence and reflect on the perennially important question, **"How can you grow in your cultural competence?"** How can *you* grow? How can *your knowledge of others* grow? How can *your knowledge of the systems* that influence choice, access, and opportunity grow? Taking the time to deeply contemplate these questions will create the right attitude and conditions for your learning and growth on the path we have invited you to walk in this book.

TABLE 1.2.   Concept Mapping Using the S.O.S. Approach

**Purpose: To visually map social identities, others identities, and the systems that impact our lives.**

| | |
|---|---|
| **Step One:** | Draw a Venn diagram with three overlapping circles containing an S for self in one circle, O for others in another, and S for systems in the final circle. |
| **Step Two:** | In the Self circle, reflect on your personal identities and write them in the circle. (e.g., female, middle-class, ci-gender, etc.) |
| **Step Three:** | In the Others circle, consider the groups you do not share a personal identity with or would like to learn more about in order to feel more competent. |
| **Step Four:** | In the Systems circle, consider larger systems that affect your life and the life of others (e.g., national policy). Also consider the mechanism where you learn about cultural others. (e.g., families and schools) |
| **Step Five:** | Reflect on the question, how can you grow in your cultural competence? How might you seek out experiences where you can learn from and interact with groups who for example are culturally or linguistically different? |

*Reflections*

When I (Noorie) have taught this activity and used similar activities with undergraduate college students who are asked to reflect on their personal identities and diversity variables, I have at times received shallow responses. Particularly, some of the white students I have taught in the United States did not initially see themselves as being diverse, cultural beings yet we all have intersecting identities. Some of those identities privilege us in certain spaces, and other identities put us at a disadvantage, depending on the context. When creating the "others" circle, participants might also feel vulnerable writing about and discussing groups they feel less comfortable with or whom they have had little contact with. When I am teaching, it may also be some of my students' first experience having a woman of color as an instructor, and I perceive that some students feel self-conscious about discussing their lack of knowledge or experience with diverse groups. That is natural and can only be countered by creating a safe space for students to talk, share, discuss, be vulnerable and have authentic conversations. I think of the groups I have personally written into the "others" on my personal Venn diagram section like a professional development plan; I use the "others" section as a roadmap for learning more and consciously seeking out knowledge and experiences where I can learn and step outside my comfort zone. Learning might be in the form of attending a talk, lecture or panel discussion, listening to a podcast, attending a creative exhibit or performance, reading the work of multicultural authors, and/or engaging in difficult conversations. As a lifelong learner, I can seek out new information, make myself vulnerable by asking questions that reflect my lack of knowledge, and seek out experiences that will help me feel more comfortable and knowledgeable.

## CONCLUSION

This chapter explored the importance of cultural competence in an increasingly linguistically and culturally diverse world. It provided an overview of the self, other, and systems model that comprise organizational structure for the rest of the book. In addition to clarifying key concepts and terminology used in this book, this chapter provided insight into the author's struggles in two contexts, struggles of learning and growing from their awareness of their own implicit bias, assumptions, and cross-cultural mistakes. These snapshots demonstrate facets of self, other, and systems understanding through personal narrative. In essence, we suggest through the sharing of these stories, that both humility and vulnerability are an essential approach and attitude when engaging within culturally different others in multi-cultural and multilingual contexts. Finally, the concept mapping learning exercise provides an introduction to the self, other, and systems approach to culturally competent engagement and models how it can be used for continued growth and learning. Culture is learned, can be unlearned, re-learned, and transformed through become fully aware of values, thoughts, emotions, and through intentional action. What follows in the rest of the book is both theory and practice for becoming culturally fluid, adaptive, and competent.

## REFERENCES:

Association of American Colleges and Universities (AAC&U). (2009). *Intercultural knowledge and competence VALUE rubric.* Retrieved from: https://www.aacu.org/value/rubrics/intercultural-knowledge

Banks, J. A., McGee Banks, C. A., Cortes, C. E., Hahn, C. L., Merryfield, M. M., Moodley, K. A., Murphy-Shigematsu, S., Osler, A., Park, C., & Parker, W. C. (2005) *Democracy and diversity: Principles and concepts for educating citizens in a global age.* Seattle, WA: Center for Multicultural Education, College of Education, University of Washington. Retrieved from: https://education.uw.edu/sites/default/files/cme/docs/pdf/_notes/DEMOCRACY%20AND%20DIVERSITY%20pdf.pdf

Barbezat, D. P., & Bush, M. (2014). *Contemplative practices in higher education: Powerful methods to transform teaching and learning.* San Francisco, CA: Jossey-Bass.

Bennet, J. M. (2008). Transformative training: Designing programs for culture learning. In M. A. Moodian (Ed.), *Contemporary leadership and intercultural competence: Exploring the cross-cultural dynamics within organizations* (pp. 95–110). Thousand Oaks, CA: Sage.

Bennett, M. J. (1993). Towards ethnorelativism: A developmental model of intercultural sensitivity. *Education for the intercultural experience, 2,* 21–71.

Brantmeier, E. J., & Brantmeier, N. K. (2015). Culturally competent engagement: The S.O.S. approach. *Peace Studies Journal. 8*(2), 4–16.

Center for Contemplative Mind and Society. (n.d.-a). *Our Mission.* Retrieved February 21, 2020, from: https://www.contemplativemind.org/about/vision

Center for Contemplative Mind and Society. (n.d.-b). *The tree of contemplative practices.* Retrieved from: https://www.contemplativemind.org/practices/tree

Cushner, K., McClelland, A., & Safford, P. (2003). *Human diversity in action: An integrative approach.* New York, NY: McGraw Hill.

Diller, J., & Moule, J. (2005). *Cultural competence: A primer for teachers and educators.* Independence, KY: Wadsworth.

*Greater Good Magazine.* (n.d.) *Mindfulness: Defined.* Retrieved February 21, 2020, from: https://greatergood.berkeley.edu/topic/mindfulness/definition

Krajewski, S. (2011). Developing intercultural competence in multilingual and multicultural student groups. *Journal of Research in International Education, 10*(2), 137–153. Retrieved from: https://doi.org/10.1177/1475240911408563

*Lexico.* (n.d.) Competence. In *Lexico.* Retrieved February 21, 2020 from: https://www.lexico.com/definition/competence

Miller, J. P. (2008). *The holistic curriculum* (2nd ed.). Toronto, Canada: University of Toronto Press Incorporated.

Spradley, J. P. (1997). Ethnography and culture. In J. P. Spradley & D. W. McCurdy (Eds.), *Conformity and conflict: Readings in cultural anthropology* (9th ed., pp. 18–25). Longman.

# CHAPTER 2

# SELF-UNDERSTANDING

The journey of a thousand miles starts from beneath your feet.
*—Lao-Tzu, Chinese Taoist*

## CHAPTER OVERVIEW

In a self, other, and systems (S.O.S.) approach to culturally competent engagement, examination of the self is a critical starting point. Self-understanding is foundational to meaningful cross-cultural interactions and vital on the long path of culturally competent engagement. Lao Tzu, a Chinese Taoist, conveyed the following over 2500 years ago:

Prevent trouble before it arises.
Put things in order before they exist.
The giant pine tree
grows from a tiny sprout.
The journey of a thousand miles
Starts from beneath your feet. (Lao-Tzu, 1998, Chap. 64)

Sometimes in popular culture this quote is translated as "A journey of a thousand miles begins with the first step." However, an alternative interpretation of the quote is one that includes examining the self before the first step is even taken—culturally competent engagement starts under one's feet. Before you take a step,

*Culturally Competent Engagement: A Mindful Approach*, pages 21–36.

look in the mirror and deeply investigate the layers in front of you. With humility, fully become aware of who you are as preparation to encounter the other. As you look in the mirror, consider the question, who am I, who really am I? Answers might include a sister, brother, or child of this person, citizen of this country, member of this ethnic, racial, or religious group, or a professional occupation. The assumption here is that in order to deeply know, accept, and respect others and where they come from, self-knowledge is a critical factor. Maybe you answer the question "who am I" with a psych-social disposition such as introversion or extroversion. Knowing the self, fully as we are, is a starting point. Yet we more deeply know ourselves from encounters with the other. A paradoxical complexity emerges here: knowing ourselves as we are is important; knowing oneself in a deeper way through encountering diverse others is vital; and seeing self through the eyes of the other can be helpful and insightful.

Rabindranath Tagore, Indian poet and Nobel Laureate, has a quote that applies quite well here, "The traveler has to knock at every alien door to come to his own, and one has to wander through all the outer worlds to reach the innermost shrine at the end" (Tagore, 1913). The point here is simple: exploring the self and deeply understanding self is a dynamic process that requires critical reflection of one's own socialization, or the influences that shaped who you are as a cultural group member. It requires coming home, examining home. It requires knowing oneself and one's own personality anew based on critical self-reflection in cross-cultural engagement processes. It requires encountering others and being open to understanding oneself more as part of the interaction. It requires engaging the "other" in a process of reflecting on one's own social identities; in other words, "understanding self through the other" (Stachowski & Brantmeier, 2002). Gazing deeper into self in our interactions within others holds the potential for transformative insight and connection.

The lifelong journey of culturally competent engagement requires transformative learning experiences that create dissonance and critical self-reflection about who we are and what we value. Honestly looking at one's belief systems and values can produce discomfort and the impetus for change. Mezirow (1994) maintains that critical self-reflection is at the heart of transformative learning. Transformative learning begins with a disorienting dilemma: a self-examination of assumptions and meaning-making practices; an exploration of new options, plans, and roles; and a building of competence toward reintegration (Kitchenham, 2008). When we intentionally place or unintentionally find ourselves in diverse, multicultural environments, we engage in disorienting experiences that allow us to question what we value, know, and perceive as true. In some instances, we see other individuals and groups for the first time, recognizing deep differences between and among people from various backgrounds.

Culturally competent engagement often results in transformative learning outcomes. Yet how do we begin knowing ourselves and the nature of our own minds more deeply? It is simple; study the self through observing the mind. Various learning exercises can cultivate greater self-understanding. What follows are three effective learning exercises we have used to help people along the path of understanding oneself as a cultural being and a socialized group member.

## LEARNING EXERCISE TWO: SELF UNDERSTANDING VIA QUIET CENTERING

*Overview*

> Awareness is to notice what is really taking place at every moment without interpretation or judgement of the mind.
> —*(Nakagawa, 2019, p. 47).*

Quiet centering, modeled after evidenced-based mindfulness meditations for cultivating self-awareness, has proven successful in cultivating calm, focused attention in the present moment and in giving rise to insight, both subtle and profound (Kabat-Zinn, 2018). As part of the process, one learns a lot about the wandering nature of the mind, habituated thought patterns, unconscious and implicit biases, and clinging and attachment to thoughts and behaviors. One also cultivates "the observer" of thought, an ability to self-regulate more in the liminal, twilight moments between thought and action. Lastly, one attunes to the responses and needs of the body when doing quiet centering. By including a body scan as part of the warm up for focused attention on the breath, embodied awareness is cultivated. This embodied awareness is quite essential for cross-cultural interactions because physical responses—positive, negative or neutral—are common when one encounters difference. Sometimes the breath becomes shallow, tension arises in the body, or a muscle or pain emerges. Sometimes the "gut" alerts us to perceived danger or harm, real or emerging from the unconscious. Paying attention allows you the ability to more freely be and choose our actions when interacting with those who are culturally different, rather than simply acting out of conditioned response.

Quiet centering has proven successful for calming, focusing, and inviting metacognition with adult learners. Our untrained minds are often distracted; they linger in the past or future, but rarely in the present moment. How are we to learn from and with one another if we are distracted by the past or future, or even by the humming of a fan in the room? Quiet centering is a particularly effective tool for understanding why and how we act in certain cross-cultural encounters. It cultivates the capacity to observe one's own mental chatter related to experience. As one practices quiet centering, we learn to understand the habits of mind—patterned ways we think about ourselves and others in circumstances—as well as patterns of emotions we experience when encountering the "other." Emotion, breath, and whole-body awareness emerge. The self-awareness gained from simply observing the mind while performing a task can be profound.

Awareness of who we are and how we were socialized and enculturated to think, act, and feel, based on interactions in various contexts (e.g. family, community, faith-based organizations, media, social media, etc.) paves the way for self-insight. Quiet centering encourages exploration of the deep questions: Who am I? and How have I been conditioned to think and act in this world? You can either read this learning exercise quietly to yourself or out loud, or listen to the recording of this learning exercise on the Information Age Publishing webpage.

*Learning Exercise:*

Learners will make progress toward:

- Calming and focusing the mind and body;
- Observing the mind and body; and
- Cultivating metacognition.

*Instructions*

- Find a quiet place, free of major distraction and where you can take a moment to begin to pay attention.
    ○ As a teacher of mine once said, be a scientist of your own experience, your own body, emotions, and mind, wherever you are today, in this moment.
- Assume a comfortable posture either sitting in a chair with feet on the floor, or sitting cross-legged on the floor, rock back and forth on the hips to help you find a comfortable seat.
- When you have found a comfortable position, set a timer for 5–12 minutes.
- As you begin to settle, roll back the shoulders to open lung capacity and increase oxygen flow. Gently tuck the chin to increase flow between the brain and the rest of the body.
- Pay attention to the sounds of your external environment.
    ○ Notice any positive or negative evaluations you may have of the sounds.
    ○ Cultivate the observer of your own experience.
    ○ If the mind wanders, gently guide it back to the sounds.
    ○ We need not force or try to control the mind, simple guiding.

- What's going on inside the body in this moment?
    ○ Sensations, emotions, distracting thoughts.
    ○ Observe any positive or negative evaluations you are currently having or that ones that are arising.
    ○ Simply notice the sensations of the body.
    ○ Notice any positive or negative evaluations you may have with the sensations of the body.

- The invitation now is to focus on the breath as it enters the tip of the nostrils.
  - Breathe in through the nose, and out through the mouth.
  - When mind wanders, gently guide it back to the breath at the tip of nostrils.
  - Breathing in, breathing out.
  - In through the nose, out through the mouth.
  - Breathing, simply breathing, just breathing.
  - Observe how the mind wanders to past, future, or distraction.
  - Guide mind back to the breath, the present moment.
  - In through the nose, out the mouth.
  - Simply breathing, just breathing, simply breathing.
  - Nothing more needs to be done in this moment, nothing less.
  - Breathing, observing, abiding in the breath.
  - Simply breathing, just breathing, simply breathing.

- As a scientist of your own experience, where are you in this moment? Body, mind, breath?
- Repeat daily for life.

*Reflections*

More often than not, it takes us some time to settle in and become calm and focused on the breath. Distracting thoughts of the past, or of the future, distracting external sounds or stimuli, or emotional distractions can bring the focus away from simply breathing. When this happens, notice the distraction, and gently, with loving kindness toward the self, guide the focus of attention back to the breath as it enters the tip of the nostrils—breathing, simply breathing, just breathing. Try not to force or control thought, but simply guide the mind back to the breath. Try to observe or ride the breath. Even experienced meditators find it difficult to stay focused—even after decades of practice—so you should be easy on yourself, now and forever.

This basic, yet complex practice can have subtle and profound effects, yet it seems important not to get caught up in too much thinking about rewards. It is important to simply do the practice, self-awareness, compassion, and insight arise in time and they also ebb and flow according to mood, rest, diet, and life circumstances.

On a more immediate level, the observation of thought, or cultivating a third person position in relationship to one's own thoughts and thought patterns, can lead to the increased ability to choose how to think, feel, and act in the world. A third person position means viewings oneself not from an "I" perspective; for example, "I" judging that person. It involves a different personal pronoun such as "he," "she," or "they" judging that person. By shifting to the third person in relationship to oneself, we create a little distance and possibility of aware-

TABLE 2.1.   Quiet Centering

| **Purpose: Embodied breathing, stress reduction, and self-regulation.** | |
| --- | --- |
| **Step One:** | Find a relatively quiet place. |
| **Step Two:** | Align body posture. |
| **Step Three:** | Pay attention to external sounds and your reactions. |
| **Step Four:** | Scan the body for physical sensations and emotions. |
| **Step Five:** | Focus on the breath as it enters the tip of the nostrils. |
| **Step Six:** | Breath in through the nose, out through the mouth. |
| **Step Seven:** | When the mind wanders, bring it back to the breath, again and again. Simply breathing, just breathing. |

ness—before action. David Levy (2016), comments on self-awareness and choice cultivated through mindfulness, stating, "In other words, by strengthening our self-awareness, we can increase the possibility for exercising choice, and thus avoiding largely unconscious reactions." (p. 32).

Quiet centering can start as a tool for embodied experience of the breath, and can grow into mindful self-regulation instead of unconscious reactions when encountering difference, such as when the body becomes tense or rigid, the breath becomes shallow. Being aware of body reactions through quiet centering sitting practices takes repetition and discipline. The practice is worth the efforts because this awareness is helpful in exercising choice in cross-cultural encounters. Your awareness of habits in physiological responses (think breath and body) can change the process and outcomes in cross-cultural interactions. The few seconds of space created by mindful attunement to bodily and breath reactions can be the difference between a cross-cultural roadblock or a meaningful connection with someone in a multicultural context. And if the mistake happens, mindfulness allows us to get perspective on that mistake, to learn, and grow from it. (See Table 2.1: Quiet Centering)

## LEARNING EXERCISE THREE: SELF UNDERSTANDING VIA PERSONAL SYMBOL EXPLORATION

*Overview*

Symbols hold hidden meaning and value within ourselves. Carl Jung, a pioneer in analytic psychology wrote, "A symbol is the best possible formulation of a relatively unknown psychic content" (West, 2020, p. 1). Deep exploration of symbols and their meanings unearths core values and habituated thought patterns, which are substantive aspects of cultural conditioning. Another tried-and-true technique for self-understanding is a personal symbol exploration that can increase self-awareness of core values, and if done with a group of adult learners, it can foster a knowledge of others beyond job titles and educational experience. This learning exercise works very well to increase self-awareness of one's core values and cultural conditioning and to promote understanding of the self in preparation to encounter the other.

Analysis of the symbols that have personal and cultural meaning allows for personal insight into who we are, how we think, what we value, why we value what we do, and how we were and are socialized. As members of communities and subgroups, we often share common values, thought patterns, and behaviors with others within that same group. Humans, indeed, are shaped and molded by the cultural contexts in which they grow. In addition, individuals vary in personality and create significant diversity within cultural groups. Fundamentally, it is important to be honest about the roots of your behaviors, values, biases, and prejudices—to see them as being created by a group of people close to oneself, and also to recognize aspects of one's own individuality.

## Learning Exercise

Learners will make progress toward:

- Exploring values and thought patterns;
- Contextualizing where values and thought patterns arise; and
- Examining how values align with behaviors.

## Instructions

Please think for a moment about a symbol that represents you. Past participants have chosen to draw scenes with people, homes, nature, religious symbols, and animals. Please do not worry about how nice or beautiful you are drawing; there is no grade or judgements on this learning exercise concerning artistic ability. Simply draw a symbol, picture, or scene that represents, captures, embodies, or expresses you. Think deeply about the one symbol that nicely embodies who you are.

After you draw the symbol or scene, physically describe the symbol in matter-of-fact terms. In other words, describe what you drew. It could be that you drew a bicycle with wheels on a roadway, so you would write that concrete, physical description. Or maybe it was nature scene with a setting sun. Describe, in concrete and clear terms, what you drew.

After the symbol or picture is drawn and physically described, explore the meaning of the symbol to you, to your family, and to your community. Consider what values and thought patterns undergird, or are implicit within, the symbol. What values does the symbol represent? For example, it could be adventure, care, belongingness, loyalty, humility, connection, or other values among a sea of possibilities. Be sure to explore the possibilities (For a list of values see Pavlina, 2016).

Look beneath the surface of the symbol to find a core value dear to you and the people who would understand the symbol as you would. Identify the value or values representative in that symbol, and write them down. Perhaps the value is family, faith, independence, connection, collaboration, freedom, community or whatever. Describe and define the value in order to communicate that value to someone else.

In the next phase of exploration, explore what thought patterns undergird the symbol you drew? In other words, what patterns of thought come to mind when you observe the symbol? What are you thinking about when gazing at the symbol? Examples might include, "knowledge is power" or "live each day to the fullest" or "blood is thicker than water" or "family above all."

Where did these values and patterned ways of thinking arise? What individual most influenced you to feel and think this way? What agents of socialization (e.g., family, religion, media, nation, etc.) most influenced you to feel and think this way? Write down what comes to mind. Then, think about some behaviors you do to enact those values on a daily basis or during special times of the year. List some of those behaviors.

If possible, find a friend or stranger, preferably someone who had completed the same learning exercise, to share your observations from this learning exercise. Physically describe the symbol, image, or photo. Share the thought patterns or core values that undergird the symbol. Sharing is a very important step in the process. Examine how you are similar and/or different from this other person. Discuss your similarities and differences and why you think this might be.

## Reflections

More often than not, the very process of drawing the personal symbol or scene and exploring the values and thought patterns that undergird the symbol often unravels layers of personality and cultural conditioning that shaped you in subtle and profound ways. When doing this activity, I (Eddie) typically draw a nature scene with trees, mountains, and a pond or a river when modeling this exercise for participants. A nature scene, upon deeper analysis, conveys my cultural value of connecting with nature, my rural upbringing, and a wide variety of outdoor activities that I engaged in growing up and continue to enjoy as an adult. I have deeply held values and beliefs that human beings need to protect nature and live sustainably, which were established from my early cultural conditioning and direct contact with a farming and outdoor lifestyle. The value of connecting and protecting nature is enacted in my daily consumer choices, such as where I buy my food (preferably from local farmers or locally sourced food) and what kinds of food I buy (preferably less processed, and all natural or organic). In other words, I try to align my core values with daily behavioral choices. Sometimes my behaviors do not reflect my core values, and this presents a misalignment, however that can potentially be a transformative moment of awareness.

TABLE 2.2. Personal Symbol Exploration

| | |
|---|---|
| **Purpose: Clarify deep values and habituated thought patterns, and their source(s).** | |
| **Step One:** | Draw a symbol, scene, or picture that represents you. |
| **Step Two:** | In writing, describe that symbol, scene, or object in literal terms. |
| **Step Three:** | In writing, reflect on the undergirding or implicit values and thoughts patterns the symbol represents. |
| **Step Four:** | Reflect on the source of these values and thought patterns. |
| **Step Five:** | Share and reflect with a stranger or friend. |

As stated above, sharing the symbol, scene, or picture with a co-learner is a critical part of the learning process. In a group setting, I (Eddie) ask participants to share their symbol/scene/picture with a partner, describe it literally, and then discuss the undergirding values and thought patterns they represent. Then, just as outlined above, they are asked to find commonalities and differences when sharing with their partner. When they introduce each other to the group, they share the commonalities and differences they discovered in the exchange.

To go deeper, you can draw more than one symbol. For instance, you could draw five symbols and deeply analyze and prioritize them according to the meaning they hold to you. Start with the most important symbol/photo/image and label it number 1. Then numerically organize the symbols (1, 2, 3, 4, and 5) according to their importance to you. In other words, visualize the five symbols as a series of concentric circles, or picture an onion with inner and outer layers. Number one would be the middle of the onion or concentric circle; the symbol that has the most significant meaning to you. When you go through the process of prioritizing the symbols, values, and thought patterns, you can gain insight into core and peripheral values. Some people have gained insight into how their values were cultivated as children and how their values have changed over time from exploring new cultures, communities, religions, countries, and/or educational experiences.

## LEARNING EXERCISE FOUR: SELF UNDERSTANDING VIA PRIVILEGE, OPPRESSION, AND POWER AUDIT

### Overview

In the book *Power, Privilege, and Difference*[1], Johnson (2006) says privilege exists "when one group has something of value that is denied to others simply because of the groups they belong to, rather than anything they've done or failed to do" (p. 21). Privilege is socially constructed, and those from privileged groups are often unaware of their advantage, which is based on certain social identity vari-

---

[1] We highly recommend Allan Johnson's book, *Power, Privilege, and Difference* for deepening understanding about the dynamics of POP; we have used it in our cultural diversity courses with great success.

ables they possess. Privilege is often implicit and the privileged are often unaware their contextual privilege. Privilege is in the air and water of social systems and institutions; it can be invisible to the naked eye unless one looks deeply at himself, herself, or their selves and interrogates social constructs that have been inherited based on the stratification and arrangement of society. Peggy McIntosh's classic article describes white privilege as an invisible knapsack—an invisible reality that acts to advantage some. McIntosh writes, "I was taught to see racism only in individual acts of meanness, not in invisible systems conferring dominance on my group (1989, p. 8). It is the invisible systems of racism, sexism, classism, xeno-phobia, ethnocentrism, and heteronormativity that provide unearned advantage. If privilege is consciously examined, one can become an ally and help disrupt the invisible social systems that provide an advantage for some at the expense of oth-ers. Johnson (2006) explains that privilege is comprised of unearned entitlements; think of these as invisible advantages one has based on a particular social identity or combination of intersectional identities (e.g., white (race), male (biological sex), and heterosexual (sexual orientation)).

An example of "conferred dominance" (Johnson, 2006) might be being a na-tive speaker of English in an English dominant linguistic environment. The fact that one is a native English speaker confers dominance on that person in that Eng-lish dominant context situation; others will naturally perceive the English speaker as "normal" and "right." In addition, being white in a predominantly white busi-ness comes with invisible benefits that provide the power of legitimacy to a white person, or the perception that he, she, or they /she/they holds the "right" kind of knowledge—not based on that being necessarily true, but rooted in how whiteness itself, in that context, affords power, currency, and legitimacy.

The flipside of privilege is oppression. If oppression is fully understood in context, one can find ways to protect oneself, develop resilience, and perhaps name the oppression in a longer process of disrupting and changing the causes of oppression and the conditions that continue oppression. Oppression can be both conscious and unconscious. Internalized oppression can occur from a pattern of circumstances and messages that a marginalized group or individuals of a margin-alized group, learn to think and feel about themselves. In Internalized Oppression: The Psychology of Marginalized Groups, E.J.R. David (2015) states:

> When we accept or "buy-in to" the negative and inferiorizing messages that are propagated about who we are, then we have begun to internalize the oppression that we experienced. We have come to learn that—having certain traits, being a member of a particular group, and being who we are—are not good enough or are not desirable. Sometimes, we even learn to hate our traits, our groups, ourselves. Even further, sometimes we end up hurting ourselves, our communities, and those who we share many similarities with the ones who likely care for us the most—our family and friends (para 2).

Internalized oppression can be related to the life circumstances that deny access and opportunity based on social identities (e.g., dis/ability, religion, gender, class, race/ethnicity, sexual orientation), institutional policies and practices, and deeper structural arrangements (i.e. economic, political, and environmental) that privilege some and exclude others. In other words, people who have socio-historically marginalized identities can psychologically internalize self-doubt and self-hate based on prolonged exposure to negative messages and challenging circumstances. Awareness of internalized oppression and how it works can be the first step toward change. Critiquing institutions and structures and practicing compassion and self-love toward oneself can be healing.

This learning exercise aims to create more consciousness about how you are privileged, oppressed, or a combination of both. Rarely, if honesty is applied and empathy cultivated, is this exercise an easy one to complete for people with privileged or oppressed social identities. Deconstructing how power operates can be a tough road. An assumption is made here that we are all privileged and oppressed based on certain social identities and combinations of intersectional identities (e.g. race, class, gender, religion, sexual orientation, geographic origin, and language) can be more salient and powerful, dependent on context.

*Learning Exercise:*

Learners will make progress toward:

- Growing awareness of privilege and oppression;
- Exploring the complexities and paradoxes of privilege and oppression; and
- Cultivating empathy for others.

*Instructions*

Let us embark on a mindful thought experiment. Look at the following table, shown below. Think through how the geographic place in which you currently live privileges you and/or under-privileges/oppresses you. You may have to go outside of your own self-perception to consider how others perceive you for this exercise. In other words, how would a stranger with different social identities view you as privileged or oppressed because of your social class, ascribed racial group, sexual orientation, and/or perceived gender identity? Reflect, in writing, under the privileged and/or underprivileged/oppressed columns. How and why are you privileged where you live? How and why are you underprivileged where you live? Write a short description under each privileged and oppressed/underprivileged category (See Table 2.3: Privileged/Underprivileged).

After thoroughly reflecting and writing down your descriptive thoughts, explore the table as a whole. Then, complete the reflection questions below in writing:

TABLE 2.3.  Privileged/Underprivileged

| Social Identity or Diversity Variable | Privileged | Oppressed/Underprivileged |
|---|---|---|
| Racial Group | | |
| Ethnic Identity | | |
| Social Class | | |
| Gender | | |
| Sexual Orientation | | |
| Religion | | |
| (Dis)ability | | |
| Language/s | | |
| Geographic/country of origin | | |
| Education status (self and of family) | | |

*Awareness Questions:*

- What diversity variables tend to complicate the privileged/oppressed columns for you? How do you interpret these complications?
- Do you feel like you are unaware of your power, privilege, or oppression as related to certain diversity variables?

*Resistance Questions:*

- Did you feel resistance, a feeling of psycho-emotive disequilibrium, when exploring a particular diversity variable? Resistance can manifest in the form of a tense feeling in the body or an experience of emotions such as fear, anxiety, anger, or a sense of self-righteousness.
- Did you find yourself critiquing this learning exercise because it brought up discomfort?
- If you felt resistance, what is the source of this resistance? What does that mean about you and how you see and/or experience the world?

*Power Questions:*

- How does power operate in these social, political, and economic contexts?
- How do you benefit from or how are you denied access in situated contexts?
- How does the context in which you live advantage certain people based on their diversity variables? Is that right and fair?
- How might others suffer or be denied access or opportunity where you live, based on power associated with their diversity variables (i.e. dis/ability, race/ethnicity, class, gender, sexual orientation, religion, language, and country of origin)?

- Have you noticed their suffering? How have you reacted?

*Empathy and Action Questions:*

- How might you build empathy for individuals and groups who are oppressed in your context? It is important to note that empathy is not feeling sorry for someone, but rather feeling with someone.
- What actions might you take to alleviate oppression and mitigate or disrupt privilege where you live?
- Should empathy be extended to the privileged? Why or why not?
- So what, now what? Is there something you want to do about privilege and oppression? Why or why not? Will you do it?

*Reflections*

This learning exercise can offer self-awareness and the beginnings of empathetic understanding for privileged individuals from privileged groups. It can offer deeper insight into the psychology of privilege and oppression and how power operates for individuals with oppressed social identities. Tensions of paradoxes and nuances clearly arise from deep examination.

This learning exercise can be done alone, but optimally, one would complete this exercise with a fellow participant, friend, stranger, or colleague. After reflective writing, we encourage verbal dialogue with other people. In this dialogue, learners have revealed complex personal stories where they simultaneously feel underprivileged and privileged at the same time. Some participants feel oppressed in one context and privileged in another. Denial of privilege is a common response; however, as Johnson (2006) discusses, just because you do not personally feel privileged does not mean that privilege does not exist in wider society, "One of the paradoxes of privilege is that although it is received by individuals, the granting of privilege has nothing to do with what those individuals are as people" (Johnson, 2006, p. 34). Privilege operates both visibly and invisibly and results in unearned advantage and conferred dominance of one group over another.

A classic example of unearned privilege is when Eddie walks into a powerful group of white male leaders in a university setting, and is explicitly acknowledged with greetings different than Noorie, a minority female. This has happened, time and time again. Eddie's racial and male privilege provides him opportunity and access to people in these kinds of rooms, and allows him to immediately have a voice in the conversation. He feels comfortable speaking up or even speaking over other white male leaders. He assumes credibility, whereas Noorie feels she needs to earn credibility in the context of powerful white male leaders. Being privileged means not having to establish and validate credibility for access and participation in certain professional and social spaces. Being privileged means reading social scenes and considering them "your space" as well. The privileged have privileged access to certain spaces, processes, and forms of power that are

TABLE 2.4.    Privilege, Oppression, and Power Audit

| Purpose: Awareness of privilege, oppression, and inherent complexities | |
| --- | --- |
| **Step One:** | Think of how you are privileged or oppressed in your current life situation. |
| **Step Two:** | Write about how you are privileged or oppressed in the boxes provided. |
| **Step Three:** | Reflect on the list of questions from the learning exercise. |
| **Step Four:** | Reflect on how others are privileged and/or oppressed where you live. |
| **Step Five:** | Reflect on your own suffering and/or that of others. What action(s) might you take to relieve that suffering? |

afforded to them, not necessarily because they earned them, but because their social identities provide them this "unearned advantage" (McIntosh, 1989, p. 6).

As social beings with group membership, all of us are comprised of inter-sectional social identities that help shape, through social experience, the "shared knowledge that [we] use to generate behavior and interpret experience" (Spradley, 1997, p. 18). Understanding how we are simultaneously privileged and oppressed in certain contexts based on intersections of certain social identity variables creates an awareness of the complexities and paradoxes of privilege and oppression. In ideal situations, privileged individuals in socially privileged groups can cultivate empathy for the oppression of others—oppression that might be very different, difficult, damaging, or debilitating for others. From this empathy, privileged individuals from privileged groups can be moved to behavioral change and action, acting as allies to confront and disrupt daily microaggressions and wider cultural and structural violence that privilege some at the exclusion of others.

We warn that the "trump game" often happens during pairing with another person or sharing as a group during this learning exercise. Individuals will make claims that one oppressed social identity "trumps" or is more important than others. Participants may think or say "I was born poor and made my own money in this world. My race or biological sex didn't matter;" or "My low socio-economic background is as important as someone's racial oppression;" or "I am a white female and my oppression matters as much or more than my white racial privilege." Though informative, these conversations can distract from the heart of this activity, which is to become more aware of one's own privilege and oppression and also learn from others and their identities and experiences.

## CHAPTER CONCLUSION

Self-understanding is pivotal on the path toward culturally competent engagement. Self-understanding requires the personal, sometimes painful, but often illuminating study of personal prejudice, privilege and oppression, and socialization. Studying one's mind, emotional, and bodily reactions in multicultural environments allows for mindful attunement and the potential for choices that lead to deepened relationships with others, relationships informed by self-awareness and curiosity about differences. In this chapter, we offered a few experiential activities to promote self-understanding as well as commentary on how and why self-understanding is an important step in learning to engage meaningfully on the path of cultural competence. With continued practice of mindful attunement to the present moment, especially when encountering the other, and by observing and recognizing unconscious/implicit bias, applying self-regulation, and examining our relationships to explore partnership and domination, we can grow in self-understanding.

In the Self, Other, Systems (S.O.S.) approach to culturally competent engagement, exploration of the self begins the journey, yet this exploration is iterative, ongoing, and dynamic. We change over time. We change depending on the contexts in which we live and our life circumstances. In this regard, our identity is flexible. Our identity is multiple, fluid, and contextual, and we have layers of cultural influences, national influences, and global influences (Banks et al., 2005). The point here is simple; culturally competent engagement takes a lifetime of observation, inquiry, and self-study. Some aspects of identity, knowledge frameworks, and values remain the same, and others can change significantly or get re-prioritized based on life experiences.

An examination of self becomes critical to deeper understanding of the other. The assumption here is that those who are self-aware on the path toward culturally competent engagement are able to discern the boundaries of perspectives and contexts of others; the hope is that self-aware individuals can deeply connect and respond to others in culturally respectful, diversity-affirming, and life-affirming ways. Self-understanding is not enough if we cannot effectively feel the world as someone who is quite different from us might feel it.

In closing, culturally competent engagement demands that we find tools to go beyond our limited frames of knowing, feeling, and doing, and consider truth, beauty, daily events, and life quite differently. We can become enriched by the myriad of diversity in our world. On this other-understanding part of the path, we often see ourselves more clearly in the mirror that another person provides for us; we see ourselves more clearly through our interactions with others. Yet this self-clarity is only a part of the learning; clearing away the self and honoring the other's beauty and bounty of difference requires emptying the self to fully receive the other—to fully learn from and with that person. In the next chapter, we will explore various learning exercises for de-centering the self and cultivating other-centeredness.

## REFERENCES:

Banks, J. A., McGee Banks, C. A., Cortes, C. E., Hahn, C. L., Merryfield, M. M., Moodley, K. A., Murphy-Shigematsu, S., Osler, A., Park, C., & Parker, W. C. (2005) *Democracy and diversity: Principles and concepts for educating citizens in a global age.* Seattle, WA: Center for Multicultural Education, College of Education, University of Washington. https://education.uw.edu/sites/default/files/cme/docs/pdf/_notes/DEMOCRACY%20AND%20DIVERSITY%20pdf.pdf

Brantmeier, E. J. (2020). Learning exercise self understanding via quiet centering final Retrieved June 25, 2020 from: https://www.infoagepub.com/products/culturally-competent-engagement

David. E. J. R. (2015, September 30). Internalized oppression: We need to stop hating ourselves. *Psychology Today.* https://www.psychologytoday.com/us/blog/unseen-and-unheard/201509/internalized-oppression-we-need-stop-hating-ourselves

Johnson, A. G. (2006). *Privilege, power, and difference.* Boston: MA: McGraw-Hill.

Kabat-Zinn, J. (2018). *Falling awake: How to practice mindfulness in everyday life.* New York, NY: Hachette Books.

Kitchenham, A. (2008). The evolution of John Mezirows transformative learning theory. *Journal of Transformative Education, 6*(2), 104–123. Retrieved from: https://doi.org/10.1177/1541344608322678

Lao-Tzu. (1998). *Tao Te Ching.* (S. Mitchell, trans.). New York, NY: Harper & Row. (Original work published 500 B.C.E. estimated.)

Levy, D. M. (2016). *Mindful tech: How to bring balance to our digital lives.* New Haven, CT: Yale University Press.

McIntosh, P. (1989). *White privilege: Unpacking the invisible knapsack.* Philadelphia, PA: Peace and Freedom.

Mezirow, J. (1994). Understanding transformation theory. *Adult Education Quarterly, 44*(4), 222–232.

Nakagawa, Y. (2019). Eastern philosophy and holistic education. In J. Miller, K. Nigh, M. J. Binder, B. Novak, & S. Crowell (Eds.), *International handbook of holistic education* (pp. 42–49). London, UK: Routledge.

Pavlina, S. (2016, April 10). *List of values.* Retrieved February 21, 2020 from: http://www.stevepavlina.com/blog/2004/11/list-of-value

Spradley, J. P. (1997). Ethnography and culture. In J. P. Spradley & D. W. McCurdy (Eds.), *Conformity and conflict: Readings in cultural anthropology* (9th ed., pp. 18–25). Boston, MA: Longman.

Stachowski, L. L., & Brantmeier, E. J. (2002). Understanding self through other: Changes in student teacher perceptions of home culture from immersion in Navajoland and overseas. *International Education, 32,* 5–18.

Tagore, R. (1913). *Gitanjali (prose translation).* Delhi, India: MacMillan.

West, M. (n.d.). *Jung and dreams.* London, UK: The Society of Analytical Psychology https://www.thesap.org.uk/resources/articles-on-jungian-psychology-2/carl-gustav-jung/dreams/

## CHAPTER 3

# OTHER UNDERSTANDING

## Appreciating and Learning About Cultural Differences

If you have come to help, you are wasting your time. If you have come because your liberation is bound in mine, then let us walk together.
*—Lilla Watson, n.d.*

### CHAPTER OVERVIEW

Do you encounter "others" with an intention to help, learn, understand, impart
knowledge, change, or be changed by them? In a Self, Other, Systems (S.O.S.)
approach to culturally competent engagement, examination of self becomes critical to deeper understanding of the "other." Understanding the other requires dis-
locating the self as the center of truth and valid experience; it requires attempting
to understand the world from very different vantage points altogether. Li (2010)
maintains,

> Following Daoist understanding, an intelligent person is empty-minded and recep-
> tive to, without prejudice, preconceived assumptions or judgement, new knowledge,
> may it be surprising or shocking. We empty our boat before we may be able to load
> more" (p. 220).

*Culturally Competent Engagement: A Mindful Approach,* pages 37–55.

"Emptying our boat" requires suspension of judgement, a profound openness to difference, and a willingness to be transformed in multicultural contexts. Emptying our boat is surely not easy—we too often hold unto our way or the ways we have been taught. Letting go of all that can be challenging and liberating.

Lilla Watson's quote, "If you have come because your liberation is bound in mine, then let us walk together" can be transformational for adults who embark on service learning projects, experiential learning, or business in the context of the "other." The quote, of course, questions the motives of the sojourner into the cultural other. Do you come to help? And what need or void does helping fill for you? Is it out of genuine concern for the other, or out of your own guilt, shame, blame, silent approval, or apathy? What is it like to feel sympathy or pity from someone else? Confronting some of these very difficult, potentially corrosive emotions is vital to moving toward deeper levels of self and other awareness.

Ethnography, simply stated, is the process of understanding and describing the culture of a group of people. The anthropologist Spradley (1997) maintains: "the central aim of ethnography is to understand another way of life from the native point of view" (Spradley, 1997, p 19).[1] In other words, a culturally competent practitioner aims to understand not from an outside point of view where one projects their meaning and interpretation onto another, but rather from the point of view of a member of a cultural group—an insider. It requires re-thinking of the Golden Rule, "do unto others as you would have them do unto you," and shifting to the Platinum Rule, "do unto others as others would have you do unto them" (Bennett, 1998). The Golden Rule can be a bit egocentric and self-centered given you assume that you know what others want and project that unto them. The Platinum Rule encourages perspective-taking and position-taking. We start by understanding another's point of view, holding our own at bay, and recognizing that both one's own views, biases, worldviews, and that of cultural "others" may be profoundly different. We strive for other-centeredness. Hanvey (1976) labels this concept "perspective consciousness" and defines it as:

> ...the recognition or awareness on the part of the individual that he or she has a view of the world that is not universally shared, that this view of the world has been and continues to be shaped by influences that often escape conscious detection, and that others have views of the world that are profoundly different from one's own (p. 5).

For some people, it is very difficult to admit the value and validity of perspectives beyond their own. Ethnocentrism and egocentrism are powerful forces that limit the ability of some groups of people and individuals to see beyond their own

---

[1] Historically, there is suspicion of white Anthropologists by some people of color, for example, Indigenous people, given knowledge acquired by early anthropologists was used to colonize and exploit Indigenous people, their cultural systems, and steal their land. Clearly, there is a racist history that undergirds the field of anthropology and the practice of trying to understanding cultural others. We acknowledge this, but also recognize that understanding cultural others through enhancing the ethnographic eye, can be used to build relationships, allyship, alliances, and mutually beneficial outcomes.

perspective and acknowledge the perspectives and experiences of others. Understanding the meaning of behavior of others requires significant position-taking with others. It requires emptying one's boat. Yet position-taking alone is not enough, inferences of meaning are required; "the ethnographer observes behavior, but goes beyond it to inquire about the meaning of that behavior" (Spradley, 1997, p. 23). Though to truly understand the methods of an ethnographer and to truly understand a culture deeply requires years, decades, or even a lifetime of immersion. However, we can cultivate an "ethnographic eye" for everyday experiences with people.

An ethnographic eye is a way of seeing that goes beyond surface level interpretation of belief and behavior. We use the ethnographic eye to inquire about values and thought patterns that undergird individual and group behavior, though it's important to note that meaning associated with a particular cultural behavior can vary across cultural contexts. On the path of culturally competent engagement, "other understanding" requires perspective taking, intercultural empathy, and skills to effectively make connections across difference and to honor diversity of experience within diverse contexts.

There are many ways to cultivate other understanding and we recommend a few promising practices in this chapter. The first learning asks you to encounter others with humility and an appreciation for their otherness. The second learning exercise encourages ethnographic observation and cultural responsiveness arising from insights. The final learning exercise in this chapter provides a tool for generating positive regard to others who you may otherwise react negatively toward cross-cultural encounters or in multicultural contexts. Please think of the learning exercises in this chapter as tools that if practiced and used over time, can help you learn better how to learn, deeply appreciate difference, and more readily connect with people who are different from you.

## LEARNING EXERCISE FIVE: OTHER UNDERSTANDING VIA APPRECIATIVE INQUIRY AND CULTURAL HUMILITY

Not until we are lost do we begin to understand ourselves.
—*Henry David Thoreau (1966)*

### Overview

Mindful humility is simple—we are limited by our own life experience. We do not know everything. We are not always right and we make mistakes. Anyone who has had a roommate or has been in a long-term relationship or marriage might quickly agree that admitting this is a sure way to peaceful conflict resolution and sustainable coexistence. In addition to recognizing that we are limited and fallible, we must recognize that the way we think, feel, and act are influenced by our family, friends, community, and a wide range of socializing forces that range from social media to the economic systems that circumscribe our lives. In short, there is more to the world than our narrow, yet important, experience of it. Thinking and feeling in another language, for example, can be eye-opening, insightful, exhilarating, and humbling.

Cultural humility, according to Hook, Davis, Owen, Worthington, and Utsey (2013) is the "ability to maintain an interpersonal stance that is other-oriented (or open to the other) in relation to aspects of cultural identity that are most important to the [person]" (p. 2). An approach of cultural humility values the inherent sovereignty of someone else and values that other people know what is right, good, and true for themselves. It is a receptive approach that fosters not-knowing everything and not projecting what we see, value, and experience onto others. It requires suspending your viewpoint and emotions in order to fully appreciate and learn about difference.

Cultural humility is an *approach* to being open. Other-centeredness is a condition of listening with intention and asking the types of questions that invite deep conversation and understanding of another's experience. Appreciative inquiry (AI), an organizational change model developed by David Cooperider, is a *way of inviting* deeper understanding of another's experience through asking powerful questions that focuses on possibilities and strengths. It is a strengths-based approach, according to Wasserman (2013), that methodologically focuses on, "elevating stories and amplifying strengths and possibilities" (p. 2). It also aids us in engaging in the world by using strengths as the starting point for relationships and shifting away from negativism and deficit thinking toward positive and affirming thinking and action.

Asking powerful, open questions to gain insight helps generate curiosity, can help stimulate reflective conversations and also serves to evoke further questions and deeper understanding. Essentially, questions formed using appreciative inquiry facilitate the sharing of stories that have the potential to build empathetic bridges. For example, if you are not Muslim and want to understand more about the practice of Muslim women wearing a hajib (head covering), rather than asking the question "Why do you wear a hajib?," you may choose, after a period of relationship building with that person, to reframe your curiosity, "How do you feel when wearing a hajib?" This simple re-framing of a question as an invitation to explore rather than an interrogation of motivation invites conversation and perhaps a story. Asking a more open-ended, feeling question invites a range of responses.

One critique of AI in regards to its application with underserved groups is the singular focus on positivity, when not all stories are positive. To fully be present and hear another person's story you also have to be prepared to hear the whole, uncensored story. As stated by Wasserman (2013) "people who hold deeply embedded historical narratives of having been marginalized, not only need to tell their story, but need their stories to be heard and acknowledged as their truth as well" (p. 2). Asking powerful, positive, open questions can be the starting point for fostering cultural humility, and appreciative inquiry can be a tool when we are open to the whole story. As stated by Brené Brown, "when you ask people about love, they tell you about heartbreak. When you ask people about belonging, they'll tell you their most excruciating experiences of being excluded. And when you ask people about connection, the stories they told me were about disconnection" (Brown, 2010).

In sum, culturally competent engagement involves a degree of humility and vulnerability. We are all limited by our own life experiences, and on the path to becoming more culturally competent, we will make mistakes. We are not always right and we will have missteps on the path. Coming to intercultural interactions with curiosity rather than judgement and asking questions that open and deepen conversations can help lead to understandings of cultural others.

*Learning Exercise:*

Learners will make progress toward:

- Developing appreciative inquiry tools for encountering difference;
- Suspending judgement; and
- Cultivating empathy.

*Instructions*

The purpose of this cultural humility learning activity is to suspend judgement, develop empathy, and cultivate an appreciation of the complexity of highly sensitive social, political, or cultural issues of our time. Find a pressing, important topic that you feel strongly about. For example, perhaps some major social or political movement like Black Lives Matter, the debate about global climate change, gun control, abortion, or current wars or conflicts. Be sure it is a topic that you hold a strong opinion about. The purpose of this cultural humility activity is to go deeply into views that may starkly differ from your own.

Next, carefully choose someone to interview and set up a meeting. For example, let's suppose I hold a strong view and concern that global climate change is one of the most pressing issues, above all others, facing the human species at present. My perception and related concern, at least from my perspective, is rooted in a strong pro-environment value orientation and is a valid and pressing concern according to some of the world's top climate scientists. Reliable scientific evidence suggests so. In this instance, I would carefully find someone with a very different viewpoint from my own, perhaps one rooted in a religious or strong economic framework, and contact that person to set up a time to meet. You may find people with strong differences than you by asking friends, fellow workers, and using the internet. Explain to the person your intent is to more fully understand diverse viewpoints on very sensitive issues of our time. Explain to them that you wish to listen and understand and that you do not wish to debate the topic. Explain you will be practicing deep listening.

Prior to meeting, develop a list of questions about the topic that you can use as a guide for conversation during your interview. Open-ended, semi-structured questions such as, "Can you tell me a bit about your views on climate change (or Black Lives Matter, or the political climate)?" tend to be good conversation starters. You might follow up with, "How did you come to hold that perspective?" or even, "Can you share a story related to the topic?" Sharing stories works particularly well because people tend to discuss in their own language and own ways what they believe, value, and habitually think about the topic at hand.

When at the meeting itself, it is vitally important that you interview without interference. What does this mean? It means you need to practice cultural humility by emptying your boat. When an idea is expressed that is contrary to your own, notice how your body, emotions, and your own thought patterns responds to the difference. This takes a great deal of awareness and self-control—to be humble, to be open, to fully receive the other and what they have to say. This is the purpose of this cultural humility activity—to train yourself to be open, receptive, and aware of thought and bodily reactions that may get in the way of deeply understanding the perspective of the other. Be sure to ask probing questions when you disagree with a viewpoint such as, "Where does that value or belief come from?" Perhaps you might probe a bit to understand if the origins of the value or belief are from family, community, religion, or the media. Be sure to disagree with curiosity and not hostility[2] to ideas expressed that are different from your own.

After the meeting is finished, be sure to thank the person for their time and the opportunity to converse. Then, find a place where you can reflect on the interview and the notes you took during the interview. If taking notes seemed odd and a hindrance during the interview and you chose not to take them, then be sure to write down your impressions immediately after the interview. Check your assumptions about the person. Were your assumptions validated or changed? Check your assumptions and reactions to the responses and interview. Compare and contrast the assumptions you had before and after the meeting.

In addition, compare and contrast your viewpoints on the topic by creating two columns labeled "My Viewpoint" and "Other's Viewpoint." What are the major points of difference or disagreement? Are there any commonalities? Taking quality time to reflect on this may provide insight into the worldview and perspectives of the other.

Finally, reflect on cultural humility and empathy in writing. What negative assumptions or judgement did you have about the other? How did you become aware of the negative assumptions or values? In other words, did you notice yourself tensing up, your breath becoming shallow, or a sense of aversion to what was being said? Were you able to remain fully open to the other? If so, how do you do that? If not, why do you think you could not? What aspects of the other person's social identity seemed to be most important for that person? Gender, race/ethnicity, socio-economic status, religion, dis/ability? Did you move to a place of

---

[2] "Disagree with curiosity, not hostility" was a guideline created by one of Ed's students during a foundations of education course at Colorado State University.

empathy, or "feeling with" the other person? Did you experience shared emotions or moments when you might have said to yourself, "Ah, that would make sense from that viewpoint?" Finally, ask yourself the question, "How can I use what I learned here in the future to practice cultural humility, or an emptying of my boat, in order to become more other-centered in my interactions? It is important to note that the purpose of this learning exercise is not to change your mind or opinion. The purpose is to open your appreciate difference, be humble, and understand other perspective in a new way.

## Reflection

On the path of culturally competent engagement, other understanding can be cultivated by being fully receptive and open to the viewpoints of others. Sometimes we need to wholly understand another person's perspective and viewpoints to have authentic dialog. Often, individuals with the same viewpoints surround themselves with people who have similar viewpoints as themselves. Deeply understanding the source of difference and more fully appreciating the context and logic of those differences is vital to open the doors of empathetic understanding—an essential element when building caring and authentic bridges across difference.

In a divided and polarized world, we need to move toward understanding the deep differences that exist. Understanding differing viewpoints is needed when you want to influence an issue or dialogue about it for the purpose of engaging minds and hearts. If you truly empty the internal chatter and bias when listening, you can fully receive the other and begin to build authentic empathetic bridges with their ways of knowing and interpreting the world. Using open ended questions as tools for appreciative inquiry can be an effective means to elicit honest dialogue, be it positive, negative, neutral, or in stark contrast to your own deeply held, cherished beliefs. Being open to fully receive the story of the other, even if might be painful, is part of the journey. (See Table 3.1: Appreciative Inquiry and Cultural Humility)

TABLE 3.1.   Appreciative Inquiry and Cultural Humility

**Other Understanding Via Appreciative Inquiry and Cultural Humility**

**Purpose: Suspend judgment and generate empathy.**

| | |
|---|---|
| **Step One:** | Explore the issue and your own assumptions about it. |
| **Step Two:** | Identify someone to interview who holds a starkly different view from you own. |
| **Step Three:** | Develop a list of core questions to ask using appreciate inquiry as a guide. |
| **Step Four:** | Interview without interference. |
| **Step Five:** | Compare and contrast viewpoints you held from before and after the interview. |
| **Step Six:** | Reflect on your practice of cultural humility and how the questions you asked were effective in eliciting an honest dialogue. |

## LEARNING EXERCISE SIX: OTHER UNDERSTANDING VIA ENHANCING THE ETHNOGRAPHIC EYE

*Overview*

Oftentimes, people enter diverse, multicultural contexts ill-equipped and without the necessary tools for understanding various vantage points. This learning exercise attempts to provide a tried and true tool for understanding and responding in a culturally responsive way. The OIIR method helps individuals who use it to develop adaptive intelligence—the ability to flexibly and fluidly respond to the observed values and thought patterns of others in culturally responsive, relevant, and supportive ways. Adaptive intelligence can be cultivated, learned, and applied on the path of culturally competent engagement.

The OIIR (Observe, Infer, Inquire, and Respond) Method (Brantmeier & Brantmeier, 2015) for culturally competent engagement has been refined over fifteen years of use in various university courses that engaged participants in cross-cultural contexts. It is a method for cultivating the ethnographic eye—an important skill and valuable tool of looking to understand the perspective, cultural meanings, values, and thought patterns of others in complex multicultural environments. The **OIIR** Method, as a tool for understanding others and then responding in culturally appropriate ways, is simple: **O**bserve cultural behaviors; **I**nfer about their meaning; **I**nquire if you correctly understand the meaning; and **R**espond in culturally appropriate ways that hold meaning and make sense to the people you are working with.

This learning exercise cultivates the ability to observe behavior, interpret that behavior from the perspective of others, and figure out if one interpreting the behavior correctly. It helps one become more perceptive, adaptive, and flexible in their work or daily encounters with culturally different individuals and groups. Using the OIIR method on an ongoing basis within daily life and/or different cultural contexts can improve one's understanding and effectiveness for connecting and working with others who are culturally different from them. The method can help to build bridges of understanding when we encounter subtle or stark differences. This learning exercise, if done well, will require significant effort and a longer time commitment than other learning exercises described in this book.

*Learning Exercise*

Learners will make progress toward:

- Observing behavior and interpreting cultural meanings of others; and
- Applying insights to respond to and to connect with others.

*Instructions*

Think about a cross-cultural encounter where you experienced dissonance. Identify social identities that are different and sometimes dissonant with your own social identities. Look back to the Privilege, Oppression, Power Audit learning exercise to identify areas of difference.

*Choosing a Service Learning Site*

Intentionally develop a plan to place yourself in the context of difference/dissonance. Local diversity exists if we look closely for it. Carefully choosing service learning sites to ensure that both the individual participant and the organization, agency, or business are mutually enhanced is an important consideration. All too often, required service learning is not supported in deliberate ways, scaffolded appropriately to a learner's and cooperating partner or site needs, and lacks preflection (reflection before engagement) and reflection during and after the experience. In shorty, they often lack structure as part of the learning opportunity. All too often service learning forays leave organizations, agencies, and/or businesses without real deliverables and impact. Often, service learning simply provides participants with epiphanies about their privilege instead of real partnership with mutually beneficial outcomes, which takes time and more long-term commitment. We warn about this from trial, error, and experience. We recommend a dedication of twenty or more hours to a single site and significant conversations with a partner, site, or agency about what they need from your engagement there. In the context of busy lives and circumstances, sometimes between eight to twenty hours of service work produces mutually beneficial outcomes.

Another consideration is that service learning can be problematic if the intentions of the participants and organization are not aligned and clarified. To avoid this, closely examine organizational mission statements, any available strategic plans, and public-facing marketing to better understand an organization and its mission, prior to inquiring about service work. You should also closely examine your own learning motivations and assumptions about the organization prior to deciding. Choosing a service learning site that will challenge the boundaries of your cultural norms is critical for breakthrough insight in this learning exercise.

What constitutes "other" for you? In this service learning activity, you should be invited outside of your comfort zone to explore difference, to challenge your assumptions, and to make "the familiar strange and the strange familiar." Do your internet research in advance. Examine the mission, vision, and strategic plan if possible. Reach out to various agencies, as necessary, to inquire about doing service learning. Choices for service learning sites can include: food pantries; homeless shelters; Special Olympics events; religious sites (mosques, synagogues, Buddhist centers, churches, etc.); organizations focused on racial/ethnic reconciliation and healing; agencies that serve refugee populations; community gardens that involve diverse populations; and perhaps agencies that teach languages to newcomers. Try to find an agency that provides mutually beneficial services and involves diverse individuals and groups of people. In instances where you choose sites with at-risk populations, be sure to abide by the rules and norms of the organization and protect the confidentiality of people at those sites when speaking or writing about them. Information gathered should be in accordance with agency policy and with ethical considerations. The basic rule of "Do no harm" should guide decisions.

### Applying the OIIR Method.

You can apply this method to intentional service learning projects that have not yet started or can reflect on an experience where you engaged in a cultural scene outside of your normal comfort zone. However, choosing a new experience will likely prove to be most powerful in terms of your learning. Here are more detailed questions to consider for each step in the OIIR Method:

**Observe:** What did you observe? Spradley (1997) breaks the concept of culture into usable bits: what people do or cultural behaviors; what people know or cultural knowledge; and things people make and use or cultural artifacts. Describe the "cultural behaviors, cultural knowledge, and cultural artifacts" that you observed in this context. (Spradley, 1997, p. 21).

**Infer:** Go toward deeper cultural understanding. What humble inferences can you make about the people and their culture/s? What values and thought patterns undergird the behaviors, knowledge, and artifacts observed? What are the explicit and implicit rules operating in this socio-cultural context? (See Figure 3.1: Weaver's Iceberg Analogy of Culture.)

**Inquire:** How did you validate your interpretations of meanings, values, and perceived rules? How do you know your interpretation is right? Did you check with a cultural insider or cultural mediator? If not, do so. What did they say about your interpretation of the meaning or values related to the behavior or artifact?

**Respond:** For this method, culturally responsive practice is understood as integrating community knowledge paradigms, values, and behaviors in meaningful ways in order to foster relevant and engaged interactions. Knowing the cultural meanings, values and thought patterns, how can you engage in culturally responsive practice at this site? How might you respond differently, in a more culturally responsive way, now that you understand more about this cultural scene?

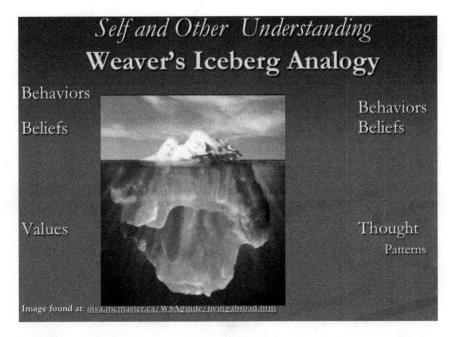

FIGURE 3.1.   Weaver's Iceberg Analogy of Culture

*Reflecting on Service Learning.*

After you finish 8–20 hours of service learning in a significantly diverse context, sit down to think and to write about your experience. Describe your observations using the OIIR method. What cultural behaviors and artifacts did you observe? What inferences did you make about the values and thought patterns that undergird those behaviors? How did you validate whether your interpretation was right in terms of the meanings of participants? Did you check with a cultural insider or with the person or group you observed and interacted with? How did you modify and adjust your own attitude, approach, and behaviors based on this new understanding of the other? Reflect on how being culturally responsive changed your experience and interaction with others.

*Reflections*

The OIIR method works well to foster insight and responsiveness. Many learners who have applied this method have reported helpful observations about a tendency to impose their values and beliefs on others. Others reported insights about how a shift in perspective and contextual understanding were fostered through applying the method. Still others have reported that deep relationships were fostered through culturally responsive practice. Participants who went outside of their comfort zones, often reported profound learning. For example, one Christian student, studying to be a school principal, attended a Mosque to understand Islam and her Islamic students better. She reflects on her service learning experience:

> I am reminded that a most important responsibility of both teacher and educational leader is to know the community that we serve. Community engagement is an important part of teaching and leading by reaching families, and understanding students. These types of experiences strengthen my ability to connect with students and community so that they feel safe, welcome, that they have an advocate, and are treated with dignity. It is my responsibility to begin to understand them, let them be the experts and teach me as we learn to know each other. This shift at times in the balance of power can be very meaningful for newcomers, language learners, members of the cultural minority, and families.

By applying this method, this student was able to take the role of the learner and approach the "other" as a teacher with insights and lessons to share. As this student demonstrates, reflection is vital to deep learning. In order to truly gain and learn from the experience, examine your assumptions prior to the experience and then after. What assumptions about people were challenged, reinforced, or transformed as part of the experience?

When reflecting on and examining your own growth in terms of your intercultural sensitivity, it may be helpful to think of it along a continuum. In particular, Bennett's (2005) Model of Intercultural Sensitivity Development has been helpful for past learners. In this model, Bennett (2005) explains that there is a continuum of intercultural sensitivity that most people go through—not necessarily in one progress-oriented direction, but rather through various stages that occur during intercultural immersion experiences. These stages include denial of difference, defense against difference, minimization of difference, acceptance of difference, adaptation to difference, and integration of difference (pp. 19–24). This progress leads toward "ethnorelativism" which is roughly defined as the acceptance, appreciation, and integration of deep differences. We can think of ethnorelativism as the opposite of ethnocentrism, where someone believes they are better than others and projects all of their values and thought processes onto others, judging them according to their own view.

When reflecting on your service-learning experience, did you deny or minimize differences? Did you accept or integrate differences? Be honest with yourself, since honesty is the only way to grow. What are your most important takeaways from your service learning experience? How might you apply these lessons to your future relationships, your work, and your engagement as a democratic citizen? (See Table 3.2: Enhancing the Ethnographic Eye.)

TABLE 3.2.   Enhancing the Ethnographic Eye

**Purpose: Observe and respond to others in culturally responsive ways.**

| | |
|---|---|
| **Step One:** | Examine your learning motivations. |
| **Step Two:** | Inquire about a potential service-learning site and look into its mission, strategic plan, and marketing to determine whether it is a good fit. |
| **Step Three:** | Choose a site that is "different enough." |
| **Step Four:** | Engage in at least 8–20 hours of service learning, preferably more. |
| **Step Five:** | Apply the OIIR (Observe-Infer-Inquire-Respond) method during and after the experience. |
| **Step Six:** | Reflect on cultural values, thought patterns, and your responsiveness at the site. |
| **Step Seven:** | Reflect on your responses to difference and your assumptions that were challenged. |

## LEARNING EXERCISE SEVEN: OTHER UNDERSTANDING VIA METTA MEDITATION FOR CROSS-CULTURAL ENCOUNTERS

### Overview

Contemplative practices from various traditions hold great power for transformative learning and insight when trying to deeply engage with and understand others. Negative associations with the "other" can manifest as physical sensations of the body and can often get in the way of authentic relationship development across cultures. In many instances, individuals react physiologically to others they perceive as not like them. This may be rooted in childhood socialization patterns of understanding the "other" as scary, dangerous, or suspicious or it is sometimes rooted in present day media images that reinforce implicit bias and prejudice; wherever it arose, most individuals have a specific other that triggers psychological and/or physiological reactions.

For example, dependent on one's race/ethnicity and gender, individuals may have a negative association with powerful women in leadership positions, black males in urban clothes, or white males in business suits. Individuals may have slight, noticeable aversion to people with certain accents or certain demeanors, or a certain kind of clothing they wear. Aversion here is understood as a strong emotional and/or physical reaction to difference. People have "psychological triggers" that initiate thought patterns, emotional, and physical reactions; in the field of psychology, these triggers are associated with past trauma (U. of Alberta Sexual Assault Centre, 2018). These triggers can be rooted in a certain stereotype or prejudice, or past experiences, some potentially traumatic, that individuals have had with people who are different from themselves. Similar to psychological triggers, *samskaras*, a Sanskrit term understood in ancient Indian contemplative practices, are the mental impressions accumulated from past experience that influence present action. This patterns of thinking are both positive and negative, and influence though, emotion, and action—sometimes unconsciously (Yogapedia, n.d.). The point here is simple; in the process of knowing ourselves and others, practice and observation are needed to become aware of patterned ways of thinking, feeling, and doing. Through practice, we can become from of habits of mind, emotion, and body.

Other understanding grows when individuals become aware of, observe, analyze, and release negative thoughts, emotional blockages, and physical sensations. Metta meditation, or loving-kindness meditation, is one of several generative contemplative practices that comprise the Tree of Contemplative Practices (Center for Contemplative Mind and Society, n.d.). Metta meditation is a simple and effective technique that can use to explore and counteract the negative responses one may experience when encountering difference. As a tool for culturally competent engagement, one can practice extending positive regard and lovingkindness to all, whether these "others" have positive, negative, or neutral associations for us.

Sharon Salzberg, a leading authority on metta meditation and a teacher of the technique for over forty years, elaborates:

> Loving kindness Meditation teaches a traditional practice for cultivating love, and applying it as a life-changing force. Dating back 2,600 years, the practice of metta (an ancient Buddhist term meaning "loving kindness") is a timeless method for unlocking your heart's immense healing resources. (Salzberg, 2015)

Several variations of lovingkindness meditation exist, depending on the particular teacher and their approach. The University of California Berkeley provides guided loving kindness meditations where you either receive loving kindness or send loving kindness (Greater Good in Action, n.d.). In terms of our approach to culturally competent engagement, metta meditation can help transform negative emotions and bodily sensations into neutral, or perhaps even positive, emotions when encountering difference in cross-cultural encounters. Openness to others, positive self-regard, and self-love are cultivated through loving kindness meditation (Salzburg, 2015, 2017). This particular contemplative practice can be generative and powerful; thinking through a care plan, especially if trauma arises, is a responsible approach. You can either read or listen to a recording of this learning exercise on the Information Age Publishing webpage (Brantemeier, 2020).

*Learning Goals:*

Learners will make progress toward:

- Generating loving kindness for self and others; and
- Applying loving kindness to negative emotions and bodily aversion experienced in cross-cultural encounters.

*Instructions*

- First, find a relatively quiet place to go inward and to focus.
- Close your eyes, or find an open expansive, comfortable gaze on the floor. Be sure to take in the entire field of vision with eyes closed or open.
- The invitation here is to attune to your body posture. Align the spine by imagining an upward pulling motion from the top of your head, perhaps visualize a string attached to your head, pulling you upward. Conversely, feel the weight of gravity pulling your body toward the earth. Notice the sensation of pulling upward and sinking downward and its effects on your body.
- Pay attention to the shoulders, gently rolling them back, if necessary. This increases lung capacity and oxygen flow. Gently tuck the chin to increase communication between the brain and the rest of the body.
- Take a few deep, calming breaths and let wandering thoughts slowly become still.
- Focus on the breath as it enters the tip of the nostrils. In through the nose, out through the mouth. Breathing, simply breathing. Allow yourself the opportunity to be fully in this moment. Breathing, simply breathing.
- Now, the invitation is to think a person you hold in high regard, someone with whom you experience warmth, kindness, and love. Picture that person in your mind's eye. What does it feel like to be with them? What emotions arise?
- What sensations arise in the body when you think of this person? Hold the person close for a while in your heart. Experience the emotions and sensations. Let these emotions envelop your mind, heart, and body. Feel the lovingkindness.
- Keeping this person in your mind, you may wish to extend the following to them:
  - May your suffering subside.
  - May you be well.
  - May you be happy.
  - May you be at ease.
  - May you experience great joy.
  - May you experience deep and lasting peace.

- Holding this person in mind, generate lovingkindness and extend affection toward them.
- Now the invitation is to think of a person neutral to you, someone who on a daily basis, you honestly do not pay much attention to. Perhaps it's a person who you know is there, but don't often choose to acknowledge. Maybe a co-worker, a neighbor, or someone that helps you at the store. Bring them to your mind's eye. Generate positive emotions and sensations when thinking about this neutral person and extend loving-kindness to them.

- Keeping this person in your mind, you may wish to extend the following to them:
  - May your suffering subside.
  - May you be well.
  - May you be happy.
  - May you be at ease.
  - May you experience great joy.
  - May you experience deep and lasting peace.

- Holding this person in mind, generate loving kindness and extend affection toward them.
- Now, think of someone you hold negative emotions toward—perhaps a person who you are suspicious of, reluctant to talk to, or recently had a conflict with. Alternatively, bring to mind a person who has different social identities (race/ethnicity, gender, sexual orientation, ability, religion, geographic origin) from yourself, or perhaps a person who has very different values than you or thinks very differently about politics or religion than you do. It could also be a person whose appearance, demeanor, attitude, accent, or bodily gestures tend to bother you. Hold this person in your mind's eye. What physical responses in the body are you noticing? What are you noticing about the breath? What thoughts and emotions are you noticing?
- Keeping this person in your mind, you may wish to extend the following to them:
  - May your suffering subside.
  - May you be well.
  - May you be happy.
  - May you be at ease.
  - May you experience great joy.
  - May you experience deep and lasting peace.

- Holding this person in mind, generate lovingkindness and extend affection toward them.
- Finally, think of yourself. Picture yourself in your mind's eye. What does this feel like? What emotions arise? What sensations do you have in the body? Hold yourself close for a while in your own heart. Experience these emotions and sensations.
- Now, you may wish to extend the following to yourself:
  - May my suffering subside.
  - May I be well.
  - May I be happy.
  - May I be at ease.
  - May I experience great joy.
  - May I experience deep and lasting peace.

- Generate lovingkindness and affection toward yourself. Wish yourself wellness, happiness, and success.
- Sit quietly for a moment, experiencing this state of awareness, this state of being human.
- Prepare to open your eyes by moving the hands, and then the feet. Open your eyes slowly, gazing downward for three mindful seconds prior to engaging with ordinary, everyday awareness.

## Reflections

Applied to cross-cultural encounters and conflict in our lives, lovingkindness meditation can provide a positive way to neutralize the negative emotions that may get in the way of wholly understanding and appreciating the diverse perspectives of others. This is important because being open and reception to others is a critical component in other understanding. When we experience triggers that result in blockages in the breath, body, and mind, we can tense up and close down our ability to "empty our boat" and fully learn from and with someone else. The practice of metta meditation can help to generate positive emotions, even to those who trigger discomfort; therefore, this can be a helpful tool for promoting awareness, insight, and growth on the path toward culturally competent engagement. Both insight regarding self and others often flows from this experience. In reflections after the experience, some participants have reported an aversion to holding themselves with loving kindness. Others reported difficulty with sending loving kindness to someone they have aversion towards. Still others reported feelings of contentment and well-being from participating in this generative contemplative practice. (See Table 3.3: Metta Meditation for Cross Cultural Encounters.) One student who participated in this metta meditation for cross cultural encounters reflected:

TABLE 3.3.   Metta Meditation for Cross Cultural Encounters

| | |
|---|---|
| **Purpose: Generate lovingkindness for self and others, and apply loving kindness to aversion.** | |
| **Step One:** | Find a quiet place and tune into the body and emotions. |
| **Step Two:** | Simply breathe. |
| **Step Three:** | Think of someone you hold in high regard. Generate positive emotions and extend loving kindness toward them. |
| **Step Four:** | Think of a neutral person. Generate positive emotions and extend lovingkindness toward them. |
| **Step Five:** | Think of a person whom you have negative regard for. Notice emotions and physical sensations. Generate positive emotions and extend loving kindness toward them. |
| **Step Six:** | Think of yourself. Generate positive emotions and extend loving kindness toward yourself. |
| **Step Seven:** | Apply positive regard and curiosity to people who trigger negative reactions in cross-cultural encounters. |

What I did find very helpful in our meditative practices and reflections in class was examining how we observe ourselves. I know that I tend to be very critical of my actions and my appearances, more so than anyone else. A big takeaway I got from that class is the importance of regularly examining my feelings about myself, and in the same way, regularly examine my feelings about others.

## CHAPTER CONCLUSION

Appreciating and learning about cultural differences and similarities requires tools for being fully open to others, even if we disagree with their beliefs, actions, or worldview. Developing tools for asking open-ended questions that focus on the positive aspects of difference, while also being fully open to hear stories of pain, sorrow, trauma, and anger, are integral to other understanding. To fully understand the positive and negative experiences of others, we need to practice suspending our own judgement and appreciating the context and source of difference. Cultivating empathy, the capacity to "feel with" others requires practice and dedication.

Acting in ways that embrace, honor, and respond to cultural differences requires an ethnographic eye. The OIIR Method provides a simple tool to observe behavior, interpret meaning, check the accuracy of your interpretation, and apply insights to connect with others in meaningful ways. Yet sometimes our biases, prejudices, negative emotions, or resulting body sensations get in the way. Practicing loving kindness and positive regard for all individuals provides us opportunities to relate to our own experiences and to others differently. This can be insightful and transformational.

In summary, we can foster opportunities to learn about others, build connective bridges, and perhaps partner with them by considering important questions:

- How do we build bridges with "others" to close the distance yet honor the diversity?"
- Am I correctly interpreting her, his, or their behavior?
- Is this interpretation all about me or really the representative of the "others" values, thought patterns?
- How might the experience of diverse "others" be understood in his/her/their current or historical context?
- How might the experiences and perspectives be understood as equally valid, unique, and important?
- Does my desire for partnership come from a place of mutual need and respect, or well-meaning pity? (Brantmeier & Brantmeier, 2015).

Though surely not exhaustive, this chapter attempts to provide helpful tools to promote other understanding. The next chapter will focus on systems understanding, a tricky, yet vital exploration on the path toward culturally competent engagement that distinguishes the S.O.S. approach from others that promote culturally competence.

# REFERENCES

Bennet, M. J. (1998). *Basic concepts of intercultural communication: Selected readings.* Boston, MA: Intercultural Press.

Bennett, M. J. (2005) A Developmental Model of Intercultural Sensitivity in *Intercultural development inventory: The developmental model of cultural sensitivity* (pp. 19–24). Yarmouth, ME: The IDI Corporation.

Brantmeier, E. J. (2020). *Learning exercise Metta Meditation for cross-cultural encounters.* Retrieved June 25, 2020 from: https://www.infoagepub.com/products/culturally-competent-engagement

Brantmeier, E. J., & Brantmeier, N. K. (2015). Culturally competent engagement: The S.O.S. approach. *Peace Studies Journal, 8*(2), 4–16.

Brown, B. (2010, June) *The power of vulnerability* [Video]. Houston, TX: TEDxHouston. Retrieved from: https://www.ted.com/talks/brene_brown_the_power_of_vulnerability

Center for Contemplative Mind and Society. (n.d.). *The tree of contemplative practices.* Retrieved from: https://www.contemplativemind.org/practices/tree

Greater Good in Action. (n.d.). *Loving-kindness meditation.* Berkeley, CA: Greater Good Science Center, University of California Berkeley. Retrieved from: https://ggia.berkeley.edu/practice/loving_kindness_meditation

Hanvey, R. (1976). *An attainable global perspective. Theory into Practice, 21*(3).

Hook, J. N., Davis, D. E., Owen, J., Worthington, E. L., & Utsey, S. O. (2013). Cultural humility: Measuring openness to culturally diverse clients. *Journal of Counseling Psychology, 60*(3), 353–366. Retrievbed from: https://doi.org/10.1037/a0032595

Li, X. (2010). Daoism, narrative inquiry, and a curriculum of peace education. In. E. Brantmeier, J. Lin, & J. Miller (Eds.), *Spirituality, religion, and peace education.* (pp. 209–226). Charlotte, NC: IAP-Information Age Publishing.

Salzberg, S. (2015, June 30). *Lovingkindness meditation.* Retrieved February 21, 2020 from: https://www.sharonsalzberg.com/lovingkindness-meditation/

Salzberg, S. (2017). *Real love: the art of mindful connection.* Bluebird.

Spradley, J. P. (1997). Ethnography and culture. In J. P. Spradley & D. W. McCurdy (Eds.), *Conformity and conflict: Readings in cultural anthropology* (9th ed., pp. 18–25). Longman.

Thoreau, H. D. (1966). *Walden or, Life in the woods. On the duty of civil disobedience.* New York, NY: Holt, Rinehart, and Winston. (Original work published in 1854.)

U. of Alberta Sexual Assault Centre. (2018, October 8). *What is a trigger?* Retrieved from: https://psychcentral.com/lib/what-is-a-trigger/

Wasserman, I. (2013). *The wholeness principle and stories of diversity and inclusion: A reflexive approach.* CW Consulting Group. Retrieved from: https://icwconsulting.com/wp-content/uploads/2013/03/The-Wholeness-Principle-and-Stories-of-Diversity-and-Inclusion-A-Reflexive-Approach.pdf

Watson, L. (n.d.). *About. Lilla.* International Women's Network. Retrieved from: https://lillanetwork.wordpress.com/about/

*Yogapedia.* (n.d.). Samskaras. In *Yogapedia,* Retrieved from: https://www.yogapedia.com/definition/5748/samskara

# CHAPTER 4

# SYSTEMS UNDERSTANDING
## Examining Societal Structures

It really boils down to this: that all life is interrelated. We are all caught in an inescapable network of mutuality, tied into a single garment of destiny. Whatever affects one directly, affects all indirectly. We are made to live together because of the interrelated structure of reality. Did you ever stop to think that you can't leave for your job in the morning without being dependent on most of the world?... And before you finish eating breakfast in the morning, you've depended on more than half the world.

—*Martin Luther King, Jr. (1967)*

## CHAPTER OVERVIEW

Systems understanding, a distinguishing feature of the Self, Other, Systems (S.O.S.) approach, requires critical analysis of context, higher-order synthesis, and deep empathy rooted in history. In short, it requires seeing current realities as a web of interconnected causes and conditions that stem from the past, manifest in the present, and shape the future. The hallmarks of systems thinking included connectedness, relationships, and context Capra (1996). Capra (1996) elaborates, "In the systems view we realize that the objects themselves are networks of relationships, embedded in larger networks. For the systems thinker the relationships are primary" (p. 37). Similarly, holistic education focuses on relationships, connections, and interdependence (Miller et al., 2019). How do relationships and networks in larger systems (cultural, economic, political, and environmental) impact individual and group experiences of those with marginalized, subordinated, mainstream, or privileged social identities? How do individual social identities or combinations of social identities free or limit oneself and others?

In an attempt to synthesize decades of thought and forge a definition of systems thinking, Arnold and Wade (2015), in the field of computer science, offer a rather positivistic yet illuminating definition of systems thinking for consideration: "Systems thinking is a set of synergistic analytic skills used to improve the capability of identifying and understanding systems, predicting their behaviors, and devising modifications to them in order to produce desired effects. These skills work together as a system" (p. 675). Arnold and Wade focus, true to a positivistic orientation, is on using systems thinking for predicting, modifying, and controlling behavior. Systems thinking and understanding can also be used to deeply understand, admire, and see how one culture's ways and modes add to the rich tapestry of diversity that comprises the human experience.

Systems thinking requires care, depth of thought, and seeing the interrelatedness of the how and why cultural values, practices, and technologies came to be. In short, it requires insight, synthetic thinking, and depth of understanding. Gardner's (2008) explains "the synthesizing mind" in his book *Five Minds for the Future*, "Against the odds, individuals seek synthesis…Such synthesis requires us to put together elements that were originally discrete or disparate" (p. 47). Understanding that an individual has a personality that can be distinct from her, his, or their cultural group, that the cultural groups has had significant influence on how a person interprets experience, chooses, and acts in the world, and that political, economic, and environmental influences also influence and shape how that person experiences the world is systems thinking. In short, layered analysis and putting the layers back together to understand the whole in systems thinking is difficult, yet rewarding work.

I (Eddie) often wonder about the causes and conditions that have led to an individual's homelessness. For example, a person might be living in a tent in the forested surrounds of Seattle, Washington in the U.S.A. for a multitude of reasons. I was recently struck by multitudes of tent camps in the wooded areas on the edges and in-betweens of highways and bridges on my way to the Seattle-Tacoma airport. At first I felt great sympathy, even pity for folks living in tents given the morning my privileged position having just left a very cozy downtown conference hotel next to Pikes Place Market. I thought it had to be cold and miserable, living on the margins of complex highways looking at the towering iron and steel edifices in the sky. I wondered how such great material wealth and poverty co-existed in high-tech Seattle. Before I judged the scene too much, I stepped away from these negative thoughts and sorrowful emotions, recognizing that the reality of rampant homelessness in Seattle would require a sophisticated look at economic systems, racial groups histories, environmental challenges, city zoning policies, and individual life histories. In short, before I went down the path of pity and sympathy, I checked those emergent emotions and understand that a deeper analysis and eventual synthesis was required to understand the situation of homelessness in Seattle from a systems lens. Appreciative inquiry and humility require of us to continually check our assumptions and habituated thought patterns when examining complex and enduring problems in multicultural environments.

Systems understanding requires seeing the interdependent nature of reality—how all things are interrelated and connected, but it also illuminates how difference and division is used by some individuals and groups of people to create dependence and sophisticated exploitation. One an also more deeply understand the causes and conditions for marginalization. Understanding power dynamics, the dynamics of dominance, and how cultural and structural violence operate through the intended and unintended exercise of social, political, and economic power is crucial for insight within systems thinking. In this regard, systems understanding involves seeing how power is wielded and how it flows within a given cultural context, thus providing tools to effectively navigate complex, power laden, cultural terrain. In addition, much can be understood about a country, society, or cultural group regarding how they treat the most marginalized and powerless within a given context.

Sometimes the cultural values and practices of a certain group challenge universal ethical imperatives and suppress larger human rights—the right to practice one's religion, to education, to health care, to medicine, to self-represent, to freely speak one's language, or to live freely and with dignity. Cultural relativism, or the notion that one should not judge another based on their own cultural standards but rather attempt to understand a cultural practice within context and from a cultural insider's perspective, is strained in situations where human rights are violated. More specifically, the cultural relativism rubs against universal human rights in these instances. Think of pre-emptive war, female infanticide, or linguistic assimilation in schools; these are all highly controversial topics with multiple viewpoints. For example, forcing people to speak English in public schools in the United States is understood, by some, as a form of cultural violence and violates the right to live freely and embody one's cultural identity. Exploring this controversial topic is imperative for deeper insight into power, privilege, and difference.

A systems understanding, in our experience, is the most subtle, profound, and challenging learning opportunity on the path toward culturally competent engagement; it is neither easy to learn nor to teach. Reading and comprehending this chapter will not be easy, but it will be worthwhile given that systems understanding is essential for deeper understanding and skillful navigation of the complexities of life in a multicultural, global world. When you see an individual or action, you intentionally *try to understand, not judge*, the causes, conditions, and connections of who or what you are observing to the larger forces within the totality of that person or group's realities in the world. In systems understanding, we see cultural actors and cultural groups within a situated, historical context and web of relations that are influenced by many socio-cultural, political, economic, and environmental forces. Understanding the web of relations within these multiple factors and influences requires perspective taking to garner deeper insight into the individual cultural actors. This allows for a more nuanced understanding of habituated thought patterns and of the values that drive thought and cultural behaviors. We see cultural actors embedded within multiple networks of interaction influenced by local, everyday realities and sometimes abstract, global phenomena

Complex systems thinking seeks to fully explicate insight into unity, with an aim to see all the diverse parts, as an essential part of overall systemic well-being. Contemplative practices serve as a foundation for cultivating insight into unity. We are all interconnected, so the assumption goes. Contemplative traditions have long lauded the interdependent nature of reality and existence. In other words, what effects some of us, effects all of us, even if we are not aware of the connections. Mindfulness with a capital M conveys this unity amid our diversity. The Buddhist tradition speaks of dependent origination and emptiness, which suggests that our reality is intertwined and interrelated, and if we look deeply into reality, we will unearth the connections of our "*inter-being*," to use a word by the Zen Buddhist teacher, Thích Nhât Hanh (Nhât Hanh, 1997). Hindu conceptions of *advaita Vedanta*, or nonduality, suggest unity amid diversity. Gandhi, rooted in Hindu philosophy, viewed reality as interdependent. He stated:

> I believe in nonduality (*advaita*), I believe in the essential unity of man and, for that matter, of all that lives…. The rock bottom foundation of the technique for achieving the power of nonviolence is belief in the essential oneness of all life (p. 390).

Gandhi's logic flows that violence against the other is understood as violence against the self from this viewpoint. The often-quoted Lakota (Native American) phrase *Mitakuye Oyasin* translates as "we are all related." The South African concept of *Ubuntu* translates as "I am because we are." A core teaching of Islamic Sufism is unity amid worldly division. These wisdom traditions, among others, point to our relatedness, our unity as human beings, and to our co-existence on the planet. These insights in these contemplative traditions point to a foundational concept in a *Mindful* approach to culturally competent engagement.

Interconnection is the hallmark of systems thinking, yet when focusing too intensely on interdependence, conflation of interdependence with uniformity and homogeneity can be dangerous. We can all be connected, yet this doesn't mean we are not profoundly different or our worldviews and life experiences are not profoundly different. For culturally competent engagement in systems to be realized, difference is essential, and essentializing everything as one is both foolish and dangerous. Interconnection and interdependence are not uniformity. Yes, we are all connected as human beings, yet not being aware of how our various social identities play out, such as race, gender, and class, in institutional, social, economic, and political contexts to provide access or to deny opportunity is nearsighted and myopic. Holding the tension between the interdependence and profound diversity is vital.

The first learning exercise in this chapter will explore how social identities are interrelated and express as privilege and/or oppression, dependent on the institutional, societal, and broader context. The second learning exercise will ask you to apply sociological mindfulness to examine the cultural rootedness of humor and joking. Through applying social dominance theory, you will be asked to examine how humor and joking serve to reproduce group identity and reinforce group superiority or inferiority. Lastly, the final learning exercise in this chapter invites readers to explore the historical context of present-day realities of marginalized groups in society. Focused on Native American history, this historical timeline analysis serves as a method to promote systems understanding and models how to educate oneself to more deeply connect with diverse others. Combined, these difficult, yet rewarding learning activities suggest that layered analysis of privilege, power, and oppression is required on the path of culturally competent engagement. Nested systems understanding of cultural others and their historical contexts is required for deeper understanding of self, others, and for culturally competent engagement.

## LEARNING EXERCISE EIGHT: SYSTEMS UNDERSTANDING VIA INTERSECTIONAL IDENTITY SHIFTING

*Overview*

We are ultimately interconnected and/or dislocated within a matrix of various social identities that influence our sense of self and how we get along in the world. How would daily interpersonal interactions, policies, and institutional practices impact you if your social identities were different? The focus for this exercise illustrates how your various social identities, come together to create experiences in the world. Yet if we change one or two social identities, dependent on the context, subtle or profound shifts of experience can take place.

Combinations of different social identity variables matter differently in nested social contexts. We, as individual cultural actors who belong to cultural groups, are comprised of interlocking and intersectional social identities, sometimes referred to as diversity variables. Banks (2001), a long-term advocate for multicultural education, provides a variety of diversity variables to consider (See Figure 4.1: Diversity Variables).

People are an accumulation and expression of various aspects of their identity, and the interlocking and intersectional identities, within a given society, influence daily social experiences and how one thinks, acts, and feels about the world. It is important not to conflate social identity with culture, which is the "acquired knowledge people use to interpret experience and generate behavior" (Spradley, 1997, p. 6). While a person's racial group or religion is not culture, the experiences of one's racial group within a broader social context, along with the morals,

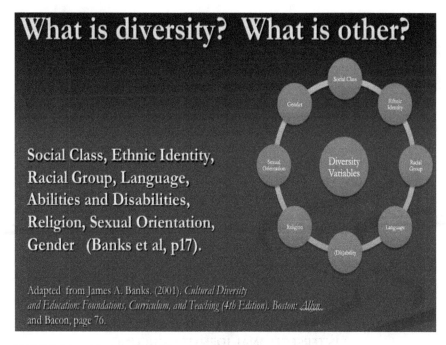

FIGURE 4.1. Diversity Variables

assumptions, teachings, and practices of one's religion, can have powerful impact on how one interprets their own experiences and how they act in the world. Social identities, within situated contexts, influence individual personality and group patterns of behavior, yet they do not necessarily determine culture. For example, a middle-class, white male's culture may vary whether he grew up in the suburbs, in farm country, or large urban city. In this instance, differences of rural or urban upbringing, educational status, and socio-economic status may have significant influences on how one white male interprets the world and acts in it when compared to other white males with different backgrounds.

The concept of intersectionality, is rooted in the visual metaphor of a traffic intersection, a place where multiple roads converge (See Figure 4.2: Road Intersection Example).

To understand individuals, cultural groups, or neighborhoods, one must investigate the intersectional nature of social identities, as well as the dynamics of the social context in which the individuals live and work. In a 2016 interview, Kimberlé W. Crenshaw, the scholar credited with developing the term "intersectionality," explains how, in the 1980s, she searched for visual metaphors to explain the "...contradictory and compounding nature" of racism and sexism within the legal system (Bello & Mancini, 2016, p. 12). She coined the term, intersectionality, establishing a helpful visual metaphor to understanding how social

FIGURE 4.2.   Road Intersection Example. Retrieved from: https://www.google.
com/ource=lnms&tbm=isch&sa=X&ved=0ahUKEwighKmF0JfdAhUwq1kKHTuvBk
UQ_AUICigB&biw=1680&bih=976&dpr=2#imgrc=1UkA5El4xBVSgM

identities come together to form privilege and oppression. For example, the social
categories of race and gender intersect in marginalizing ways for women of color
in relation to housing and employment in the United States. To study and deeply
understand this, one needs to examine the intersections of these social identities
(or diversity variables).

An additional metaphor used to describe intersectionality is a "matrix of domination" (Collins, 2000). In her work, rooted in African-American and feminist
studies, Patricia Hill Collins describes how racism, classism, and gender form an
interlocking system that combines multiple forms of oppression with stifling and
marginalizing results. For example, in a white male dominated society, a poor,
African-American woman's advancement may not only be stifled by institutional
policies and practices that favor men, but she may also face challenges and obsta-
cles of racism and sexism, both visible and invisible. This is because institutional
norms and practices may mirror that of middle-class, white males. Institutional
policies may favor whites over people from other racial groups. Institutional culture may value fierce competition and dominating discourse in business meetings
and in social interactions. As seen in this example, the matrix is the interconnected
web of oppression that can serve to further marginalize based on social identity
categories—such as race, class, and gender. The point here is that understanding
social identities and how they matter in various cultural contexts requires an intersectional and systems understanding. When gazing into the prism of one's identity, we understand that individuals refract multiple social identities that comprise
a more whole rendition of their experienced social and material reality.

*Learning Goals*

Learners will make progress toward:

- Understanding how the intersection of social identities deepens privilege or oppression in situated contexts; and
- Practicing position-taking to determine how privilege and power operate in regards to the intersection of social identities.

*Instructions*

How does a larger cultural system impact individuals with marginalized, subordinate, mainstream, or privileged social identities? If we look at our racial or ethnic group, social class, gender, religion, language (mother tongue), place of employment, country or geographic region of origin, educational background, dis/abilities (both visible and invisible), and sexual orientation, we may find similarities or differences when we compare them to people who are different from us. So, how does a difference in social identity impact one's experience in the world of work—socially, politically, or economically? What is the experience of a transgender person who needs to go to the restroom in public? How does a woman feel when she needs to walk across a dark parking lot to get to her car at night? How does a person of color feel when they need to go to the bank to ask for a loan to purchase property or when they arrive at an election site for voting? What is it like for a person using a wheelchair to plan for an international work trip? What is it like for a person in a non-dominant religion to ask to take off work for a special religious gathering?

You can begin to see how applying these questions to yourself and taking the position of others can help you practice other understanding. If you are a Christian, what would it be like to be Buddhist, Jewish, or Muslim in a Christian dominate community? If you are white, what would it be like to work within a predominantly black community? This line of questioning creates awareness about how various aspects of your identity, in social or business contexts, influence and help shape your experience. One, two, or three small changes in social identity could subtlety or profoundly change your sense of self, your agency to do what you wish, your access, or your opportunities.

*Map Your Social Identities*

The first step of this activity is to make a list of your social identity variables, or alternatively, use the Intersectional Identity Map provided. For example, Eddie would write the following: white (racial group); middle class (social class); male/masculine (sex/gender); Buddhist-Catholic-Quaker (religion); English speaking plus Spanish conversational (language/s); university professor (occupation/place of employment); USA/Wisconsin raised (country/geographic origin); first-generation college student, now Ph.D. (educational background); and able-bodied (dis/ability). Noorie, would write something like the following: Native American/ Black Puerto Rican (racial group); middle class (social class); female (sex/gender); not religious (religion); English speaking (language/s); university professor (occupation/place of employment); third-culture kid (country/geographic origin); first-generation college student, now Ph.D. (educational background); and able-bodied (dis/ability).

Now, write down your answers to these categories. Think of your identities as an intersection on a street. Perhaps it is a four-way intersection or a roundabout. Use a blank sheet of paper and draw a small circle in the middle with various roads coming into the circle, as shown below. Write your name in the circle. Then draw various lines coming into the circle. Write your various social identities on those lines (or roads) (See Figure 4.3: Intersectional Identity Map).

This is an intersectional identity map of who you are. You are the inner circle of a roundabout with multiple social identities comprising who you are.

After you create a complete map of the intersection of your social identities, choose three that are most salient or important to you. Perhaps they are religion, social class, and racial or ethnic group, or perhaps they are gender, religion, and language (mother tongue). This is a highly individual and personal activity—only you can decide based on your sense of self and your social experience. After you choose two or three identity variables that are most important to you, reflect on your everyday experiences, which may include the following:

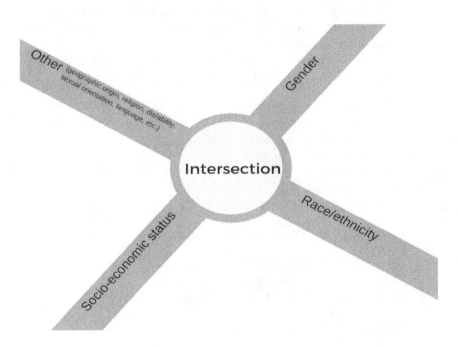

FIGURE 4.3. Intersectional Identity Map

- Going to the bathroom in a public place;
- Going to the doctor or hospital;
- Going to vote;
- Being at work; and
- Going to the bank to open an account.

Now reflect on what these experiences are like for you.

- How do you feel when doing everyday tasks?
- How do people treat you or react to you in these contexts?
- What is a normal way people respond to you? What would be an abnormal way? What larger cultural forces, such as stereotypes, prejudices, or discriminations, impact your experience?
- What institutional policies are in place to advantage or disadvantage your progress?
- What cultural norms and practices are accepted in this context?

### Shifting Your Intersectionality

Now, shift your identity. Replace the three most important aspects of your identity with choices that you perceive to be most different from you. Mark a line through what you previously wrote and write a new identity next to it. For example, Eddie (white, heterosexual, male,) might choose to replace his racial group with African-American, his sexual orientation with gay, and his biological sex with female.

After you make your concrete choices or shifts in identity, slow down and experience the shift. Then, reflect on the same everyday experiences again, through a new lens.

With this identity, what is it like:

- Using the restroom/ bathroom in a public place;
- Going to the doctor or hospital;
- Going to vote;
- Being at work; and
- Going to the bank to open an account.

Now reflect on what these experiences are like for you.

- What are your experiences in these various contexts like now?
- How do you feel? What do you think?
- How do you get along with others? How do people treat you or react to you in these contexts?
- What is a normal way for people respond to you? What is an abnormal way?

- What larger cultural forces, such as stereotypes, prejudice, discrimination, impact your experience?
- What institutional policies are in place to advantage or disadvantage your progress? What cultural norms and practices are accepted in this context?
- If you are having a difficult time imagining what it might be like for someone different than you, what does this convey? How might you remedy not knowing about the experiences of diverse others?

## Systems Thinking and Social Experience

Take some time to reflect on the different layers of a system (i.e., personal, interpersonal, institutional, societal, economic, political, and environmental). Make this learning exercise more personal by thinking of a few friends or people who have different social identities in comparison to you—people you know on a more personal basis. Contemplate the following questions to complete this learning exercise:

- What are their experiences like?
- What barriers or opportunities do they encounter based on social or economic realities, without even trying?
- How might changes in cultural norms, institutions, and society create access, opportunity and allow people to live freely and with dignity?
- What is your most important takeaway from engaging in this learning exercise?

## Reflection

The intersection of various social identities increases or reduces one's privilege and oppression; typically, this is context dependent and is related to how power operates and the dynamics of dominance: how forces work together to allow one group to control another group within that context (Howard, 2006). Reflecting on the parts that comprise one's identity, and seeing how social systems privilege or oppress individuals based on a combination of intersectional identities, is vitally important in this activity. Personal, interpersonal, social, and institutional experience are undoubtedly influenced by existing systems of privilege and oppression. Being aware of one's own privilege and oppression, and that of others with whom we interact, creates a sensitivity in cross-cultural contexts that allow for deeper insight and empathy.

As previously stated and explored in this book, awareness can be cultivated through contemplative practices. Contemplative practices such as basic mindfulness meditation foster awareness of one's own positionality. Metta meditation can cultivate positive regard and empathy for people we may experience aversion toward. We can learn to monitor and generate positive emotions toward people we may judge or distrust. The previous intersectional identity shifting learning exer-

TABLE 4.1.    Intersectional Identity Shifting

| | |
|---|---|
| **Purpose: Understand Intersectional identities and empathize with others.** | |
| **Step One:** | Make a list of your social identity variables. |
| **Step Two:** | Reflect on your everyday experiences (such as going to the bathroom, going to the hospital, going to vote, being at work, going to the bank). |
| **Step Three:** | Shift three identities. |
| **Step Four:** | Reflect on your everyday experiences with these hypothetical identities. |
| **Step Five:** | Reflect on identities and how systems privilege some and oppress others. |

cises asks you to actively imagine the world as if your identities were their identities. Thinking of how it might feel to be privileged or oppressed if your identity shifts can open doors for understanding the experience of others and help cultivate intersectional empathy. Intersectional empathy, as defined here, is the ability of an individual to understand privilege or oppression based on experiencing them with one or more of their own social identities. For example, someone may not personally experience oppression based on their sexual orientation, yet they understand racial oppression. In turn, a basic intersectional empathy is cultivated and extended to people oppressed based on their sexual orientation. Intersectional empathy builds bridges of understanding between and among people with diverse social identities. Race/Ethnicity may be extended to the oppressed other based on sexual orientation. To know what it feels like and to know how systems of oppression operate can be powerful connectors.

Understanding of intersectionality can lead to empathy and broader insight into social systems and how power operates within them. Is it possible to move away from "power up/power down" relationships and create "power with" and "power within" relationships and policies? (Brantmeier, 2013). Tuning into the power dynamics of a social context allows one to make different choices of how to disrupt unfair and unjust power relationships, or become an ally to others who experience marginalization. Being a supportive ally will be discussed with more depth in the concluding chapter to this book. (See Table 4.1: Intersectional Identity Shifting.)

## LEARNING EXERCISE NINE: SYSTEMS UNDERSTANDING VIA SOCIOLOGICAL MINDFULNESS

*Overview*

Systems understanding requires seeing how the micro (i.e., personal and/or familial) is connected to the macro (i.e., institutions and/or society). Schwalbe (2005) writes of sociological mindfulness, a helpful tool for our self, other, and systems approach and states, "Mindfulness is useful because it helps us see how our lives are intertwined and how our words and deeds help or harm others in nonobvious ways. Being sociologically mindful is especially important for helping us see that the consequences of our words and deeds often escape our intentions" (p. 4). Everyday words and deeds reinforce or disrupt larger narratives about the power and position of one's group and others' groups, about those who are oppressed or maintain privilege amid explicit and implicit power hierarchies. Individuals and groups all have "others" they view as lesser or greater. In this sense, individual thought and action have larger institutional and social consequences.

Unconsciously, social inequalities are reproduced by perpetuating, rather than contesting or disrupting, narratives about the "other." Why do people create "other" groups that are lesser or better than one's own? What deep need does it satisfy? How does this othering process work? This learning exercise explores some of these questions. Often where people were born and grew up, there were "legitimizing myths" that reinforced one's superiority or inferiority in relationship to others (Sidanius & Pratto, 1993). These legitimizing myths may have come in the form of prejudicial statements made about others. Sometimes jokes or stories are shared and passed down from parent to child, from teachers to students, from elders to young ones, from generation to generation.

Examining the social function that humor and jokes about others serve can be particularly revealing. Typically, these jokes or stories create borders between "us" and "them"; they reinforce feelings of superiority or explain realities of real or perceived inferiority. On a wider scale, groups of people or governments sometimes use media campaigns, employing legitimizing myths that denigrate and dehumanize groups of people within a society. Think about the legitimizing myths used in colonization of Indigenous people all over the world; or how Apartheid worked in South Africa, or about the rise of Nazi Germany; or the American war in Vietnam; or contemporary struggles against radical Islamic terrorist groups that get twisted into Islamophobia; or the contemporary political divisions in the United State. "Us and them" borders are maintained not only by walls and barbed wire, but also by everyday stories and jokes told about those on the other side of the wall.

Social dominance theory, a powerful explanatory tool, maintains that social hierarchies (i.e., privileged vs. underprivileged groups, powerful vs. weak groups, better vs. lesser groups) are reproduced through intergroup oppression on individual and institutional levels (Sidanius, Pratto, van Laar, & Levin, 2004). Everyday norms get institutionalized into policy and practice and systematically deny equity and inclusion to some. Elaborating on what their theory aims to explain, Sidanius, Pratto, van Laar, & Levin (2004) state, "...social dominance theory is explicitly devoted to trying to understand how psychological predispositions, social identities, social context, social institutions, and cultural ideologies all intersect to produce and reproduce group-based social inequality" (p. 849). The image that follows illustrates the layers of social dominance theory (See Figure 4.4: Intersecting Layers of Social Dominance Theory).

# Social Dominance Theory
## (Sidanius, Pratto, van Laar, & Levin, 2004)

FIGURE 4.4. Intersecting Layers of Social Dominance Theory

The image nests the individual within social layers of influence that work together to tell positive or negative stories about "us" and "them"—their in-group and out-groups. Exploring common jokes within an in-group (i.e., family, community, cultural group) is one way to examine how social dominance is reproduced through everyday interactions. Overtime, when people are ongoingly dehumanized, lower status, inferiority, and inequality are easier to explain away. Social dominance theory aims to describe social inequality and how it is reproduced on individual, institutional, and macro-cultural levels. Concrete examples of how inequality is reproduced are offered in the quote that follows:

> That is, many social institutions (e.g., schools, organized religions, marriage practices, financial houses) and many powerful individuals disproportionately allocate desired goods—such as prestige, wealth, power, food, and health care—to members of dominant and privileged groups, while directing undesirable things—such as dangerous work, disdain, imprisonment, and premature death—toward members of less powerful groups. (Sidanius, Pratto, van Laar, & Levin, 2004, p. 847)

Allocations of prestige to certain jobs (such as entrepreneurs, doctors, lawyers, CEOs as "good" jobs) are socially embedded. Allocation of "undesirable" jobs (such service jobs, road crews, night shifts) are socially constructed. These social creations help maintain power hierarchies and systems of privilege and oppression, and the economic system reinforces this. Different wages are earned for desirable and "undesirable jobs" in U.S. society for example. The material conditions of some are abundant and those who have "undesirable jobs" sometimes others suffer greatly from day to day to make rent, buy food, or pay off medical bills.

This learning exercise explores how *seemingly* harmless jokes about race, gender, and poverty uphold deeply entrenched structural inequality and violence against people of color, women, and poor people in the United States or other countries. There is an assumption that should be tested here; individuals all are raised with harmful narratives of "others" that reinforce and maintain boundaries and borders of "us" and "them." The following activity asks readers to see how beliefs about others, expressed through common jokes, may help to reinforce the norms of cultural groups and then institutional policies and practices. Simple, everyday humor can be harmful and helpful for the reproduction of inequity and inequality if examined on deeper levels.

## Learning Goals

Learners will make progress toward:

- Examining personal beliefs that may be harmful or helpful to others; and
- Connecting personal belief and practice (micro) to the perpetuation or disruption of institutional inequality and structural violence (macro).

## Learning Exercise

Humor and joking are culturally rooted, meaning they are sometimes funny to in-group members of a culture and the way they make meaning, and not so funny to others. Social norms are reproduced through jokes about others. For example, think of a joke that your family or people in your community told about others when you were growing up. This may be a positive or painful experience because jokes can uncover some raw and ugly truths about the legitimizing myths people around you told to make themselves feel superior or to explain lower status positions—for whatever reasons. Be honest. These jokes may be about people from another place, such as immigrants, or they may be people of another religion, or individuals who spoke a different language, or people from another neighboring country, or people who lived in a different part of town. If you are unable to recall a joke, ask a friend, family member, or neighbor about a joke about the "other." Perhaps it is a group of people who live in another place, another country, another part of the world—explore a little bit.

Using sociological mindfulness to see how the everyday-enacted larger layers of institutional or structural inequality, think of how jokes helped or harmed other individuals and groups of people. Think of a joke that the cultural group to which you were born told about other groups of people. Write the joke on a piece of paper or on a computer. Be honest, in the spirit of inquiry. Given the severity of negativity of the joke, it can be hard to be honest, to yourself and to others, that this joke may have been told in your family or in your community. It is best to pick a joke that comes from home. However, if you are unable to think of one, do a quick internet search using the search terms, "racist jokes." Find one that is suitable for the activity. Perhaps it is a joke that is about the intelligence or laziness of another group of people.

For example, I (Eddie) grew up on mostly German-American northeastern Wisconsin farming country in the 1980s and 90s. There were many negative jokes about people with Polish descent, people who lived just north of where I grew up. "How many "Pollocks" does it take to change a light bulb? Four, one to hold the light bulb and three to turn the ladder." People would laugh, offer another joke about Polish people, and then go on with conversation, as if denigrating others was ok and a natural part of conversation.

Think of your own family or community jokes. Perhaps those jokes were about people with different hair color (blondes) or skin color (brown, black, mixed, or white people).

### Social Identities and Context

Examine how the "others" portrayed in the joke were different from you.

- How were they different in terms of skin color, language, religion, sexual orientation, gender, geographic origin, etc.?
- How did this joke help maintain, reinforce, or create boundaries, barriers, or borders between "us" and "them"?
- Were there actual physical or geographic barriers between your group and this group? Explore and explain.
- Applying sociological mindfulness, what function did this joke serve for your group? Who benefited and who suffered? What were the implications of the joke on the "other?"
- Who benefited and who suffered based on the arrangements of "us" and "them"?
- How did/does the joke promote inclusion and exclusion?

### Social Institutions

Now explore the wider societal implications of the joke.

- Did some of the tensions between or among groups show up in institutions?
- In the policy and practices of local businesses or geographic space?

- Who are/were the people in power? What "culture of power" (Delpit, 1988) operated in these institutions?
- What people, from what groups, were in power?
- Who established and reinforced the rules? What about how neighborhoods were designed or segregated?

## Cultural Ideologies

Jokes can serve to reinforce cultural ideologies, or the group stories that an in-group tells about others.

- What story is being told about the cultural others and what are implications of that store, as they reinforce ways of thinking about, feeling towards, or interacting with others who are different from you and your cultural group?
- How does the joke or jokes connect or reinforce systems of beliefs, ideals, and assumptions about what is right, true, just, and sensible for a group of people?
- How does the humor reinforce inclusion, exclusion, connection, or oppression?

This may be a difficult task to make the connections, so if that is the case, then think of a different joke that can more clearly illustrate how humor and joking can serve to reinforce positive and negative group identities.

## Reflection

Cultural violence, simply defined, is enacted through in-group norms that help to perpetuate direct or indirect violence against others. Seemingly harmless jokes are the foundation or building blocks for dehumanizing others, and they help to perpetuate legitimizing myths about conditions of inequality. For example, "if only those people would work more and not be so lazy, they would not have to drain the social welfare system." Are there deeper cultural ideologies and political and economic structures at play in creating conditions of poverty and resource disparities?

The stories told by in-group members have powerful prejudicial and galvanizing effects and help maintain the borderlands of us and them. They protect and uphold in-group norms, behaviors, and power imbalances by devaluing others. Sociological mindfulness can be applied to how personal beliefs, inherited from family and community socialization, can help reproduce larger systems of inequality. For example, legitimizing myths can reinforce institutional racism, sexism, or classism, such as, "those people are just dumb and lazy; women are too emotional and cannot lead people and governments; and rich people are rich because they are simply smarter than poor people." Meant to be funny, some jokes simply promote prejudice and serve to justify structural inequality and cultural violence. These beliefs lead to inclusion of some and exclusion of others—in job

TABLE 4.2. Sociological Mindfulness Activity

**Purpose: Examine how social dominance is perpetuated between/among groups though joke telling.**

| | |
|---|---|
| **Step One:** | Think of joke from your family or community. Write it down. |
| **Step Two:** | Examine how the joke portrays "others." |
| **Step Three:** | Examine how this portrayal reinforces power dynamics between or among groups, how it reinforces inclusion and exclusion. |
| **Step Four:** | Consider the positive and negative consequences of the joke in institutions, society, economic, and political systems. |
| **Step Five:** | Apply sociological mindfulness in daily interactions when encountering jokes or stereotypes—how are your thoughts and speech acts connected to power, inclusion, exclusion, liberation or oppression. |

choices, healthcare, social groups, and institutional policies and practices. Sociological mindfulness asks us to question beliefs and their sources. Sociological mindfulness asks us to see how these beliefs reinforce or disrupt larger inequalities. Sociological mindfulness asks us to be aware of our own habituated ways of thinking, feeling, and acting, and asks us to examine their source, their roots, and question how these influences help to promote connection or oppression (See Table 4.2: Sociological Mindfulness Activity).

## LEARNING EXERCISE TEN: SYSTEMS UNDERSTANDING VIA HISTORICAL TIMELINE ANALYSIS

### Overview

The historical past impacts present day realities for individuals and groups of people. Which groups of people hold power in our society? Who has access to the best resources? Which policies and practices give some members more direct access to opportunity? Who gets to live in safe, secure housing? Who is able to ensure that their children have an education that prepares them for their futures? These are just a few questions to start the discussion about how a deep, systemic understanding of history can increase one's capacity for deeper connection during culturally competent engagement. Examining the context and experience of diverse groups in the United States and across the world sheds light on how the present-day experiences of diverse groups are connected to a historical past.

In the United States, for example, past federal policies have legitimized and given white, male property owners privileged access to resources, wealth accumulation, and the ability to pass on that wealth generationally. On the other hand, historically marginalized groups, such as Native Americans, African Americans and Latinos, have had land, wealth, and opportunity systematically stripped from their communities through governmental policy and educational systems (Spring, 2010). In examining present day realities of marginalized groups of people through the lens of systems understanding, the historical context of power, oppression, and privilege can be more fully understood. There is a legacy of privilege, rooted in history and context that must be examined. Understanding this historical context is necessary for deeper engagement with the learning exercise that follows.

For example, for centuries, the U.S. government created much of its wealth by appropriating Native American lands and forcing its Indigenous people onto reservations as part of the 1830 Indian Removal Act (Wilkins & Stark, 2011). Additional lands were taken through the 1887 General Allotment Act, which allowed the U.S. government to assume nearly 90 million acres of Native lands without compensation. The lands taken by the U.S. government were then redistributed to white settlers through the Dawes Act. The policies referenced, though instituted long ago, have a substantive impact on the economic circumstances of tribal communities in the United States, especially when you consider the present-day cost of land per acre. In the 1940s, in an effort to assimilate Native Americans into American culture, over 100 tribes were terminated and another 2.5 millions of acres were lost. Decades of intentional U.S. governmental policies stripped Native people of their land and resources, creating a racial wealth divide between them and White Americans. This is a classic example of institutionalized racism through public policy that stripped wealth from Native American people.

Today, due to historical practices of wealth stripping and discriminatory practices, Native Americans stand with African Americans and Latinos on the asset-poor side of the racial wealth divide, with Native Americans experiencing the highest poverty rates across all racial groups. It is important to note that tribal nations are diverse; with over 570 federally recognized tribes and more than 240 state-recognized tribes, some have been quite successful in exercising their sovereign nation status to increase wealth and economic development opportunity for their citizens. However, on average, Native people continue to experience some of the highest poverty rates, highest levels of health disparities, lowest life expectancy, lowest educational levels, and multiple housing-related disparities nationally. To provide a bit of context about current Native American community challenges, consider the following statistics:

- 25% of Native American children live in poverty;
- 3/5 of Native American women will be assaulted in their lifetime;
- Native Americans are 38% more likely to experience accidental deaths;
- Native Americans are 126% more likely to have liver disease and cirrhosis;
- Suicide rates in Native communities are more than 3X the national average, and in some communities, up to 10X; and
- Native Americans are 38% more likely to be incarcerated. (Indian Health Service, 2019; U.S. Census Bureau, 2017)

Wealth stripping policies leading to decreased access to resources, paired with systemic efforts to assimilate Native people, have led to multiple negative social issues. On the converse, despite the challenges mentioned above, there is a rising tide of Native leaders exercising self-determination as a tool for economic and community development. Native communities are using the system, or legal channels, to regain compensation for lost tribal lands and assume control of the administration of vital tribal programs, such as health and human services.

The previous examples from U.S government policy and its consequences Native-American communities demonstrates the way historical events and policies, or a system of structural racism and discrimination, impacts present-day realities. Understanding and learning about the past and hearing the counter-narrative history from the viewpoint of marginalized individuals and groups allows for deeper awareness and cultural competence to emerge (Brantmeier, Aragon, & Yoder, 2009).

*Learning Goals*

Learners will make progress toward:

- Identify and analyze historical events in U.S. federal policy and Native American history that contribute to current day poverty and lack of resources.
- Use the process of examining Native American history as a case example and consider ways historical timelines can be used to situate the experience of other marginalized groups within a historical past (e.g., women, African Americans, LGBTQ+, Latinx)
- Reflect on the ways historical contextual understanding increases an individual's effectiveness in cross-cultural encounters.

*Learning Exercise*

To better understand and explore the way systems and policies impact the lives and experiences of diverse groups, creating a historical timeline can be a useful tool to see connections between the past and present. Past federal policies, key events in history, social movements, technological innovations, and cultural shifts impact our present-day experience. Understanding historic events in a chronological progression can shed light and give greater context for a marginalized group's experience and the impact of systemic disadvantage over time. For the purpose of this learning exercise, we will focus on the history of Native American people in the contexts of the United States government's policies and practices.

To begin, consider some of the statistics presented above regarding current Native American community challenges. In Figure 4.5, you will find a presentation called, "Timeline of Key Periods and Historic Events in Native American History: Pre-1492 to Present." This presentation was developed as part of Seven Sisters

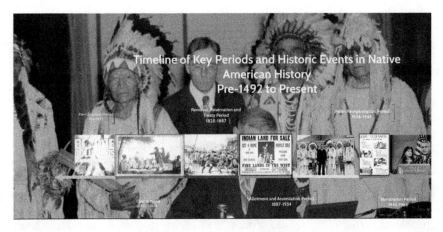

FIGURE 4.5.   Historical Timeline Presentation. Retrieved from: https://prezi.com/
k0ltuxvdxl1u/timeline-of-key-periods-and-historic-events-in-native-american-history/

Community Development Group's work providing foundational knowledge about the historical context of tribal communities to investors, foundations, federal government partners, and others who want to engage with tribal communities. Begin this exercise by moving through the Prezi and watching the embedded video. As you view the presentation, summarize and make note of policies practices, or systems that impact present-day poverty in Native American communities. Unequal wealth distribution and less access to resources has led to multiple social challenges in Native American communities. What connections are you able to make between the historical past and current realities? (See Figure 4.5: Historical Timeline Presentation.)

Now consider the history of a different group in society, perhaps women. What policies, practices, or systems impact current reality, especially considering that men disproportionality lead Fortune 500 companies, most often in senior leadership positions. To become more culturally competent, we must individually understand and be reflective of our own experiences in order to include the ways in which we are privileged and underprivileged, depending on our intersectional identities. We must engage with others through a lens of curiosity, devoid of judgement, and through open conversations in order to build cross cultural understanding. Additionally, we must understand the current realities of marginalized groups within the context of a historical past that has systematically privileged some groups at the expense of others.

*Reflections*

The Native American timeline activity is one that I (Noorie) have done as a consultant and in my role as a university faculty member. I have also adapted this activity to simultaneously review key events in the histories of multiple marginalized groups. In groups, training participants then co-constructed a timeline in order to see patterns of discriminatory policies and practices beside rising trends of activism and movements for social justice and equality. When doing the Native American timeline activity, due to a lack of knowledge about Native American history in K–12 education in the United States, most mainstream students and training participants are shocked at the aggressive attempts by the U.S. government to systematically oppress Native people. When thoughtfully considering the long-term impact of harmful policies and practices over time on Indigenous people and other marginalized groups, mainstream students often emerge angry about what they have been taught, sad, or simply wanting to do something about injustices.

Consider the long-held belief in American culture that with enough hard work everyone can get ahead, or the belief that everyone has equal access to the American dream—the myth of meritocracy. But is this true for all people? When examining this belief, I often think of the game *Chutes and Ladders*, a game I play with my six-year-old son. We start on the game board and roll the dice to move our character. Depending on the space you land, you may get a ladder that gets you to the finish line more quickly, or you might land on a chute where you are quickly taken further away from the finish line.

In our real game-of-life, some groups systematically land on a chute that sets them back or makes them take the long way around, while others have been systematically privileged to help them land ladders that speed them toward success. For example, a person will encounter more *ladders* if they are a white, educated, English-speaking male, from a high socioeconomic status. A person may encounter more *chutes* if they are a person of color, a female, LGBTQ+, come from a low socioeconomic status, are an English-language learner, and/or have a disability.

TABLE 4.3.  Historical Timeline Activity

**Purpose: To situate the experiences of diverse groups in a historical context.**

| | |
|---|---|
| **Step One:** | Review the historical timeline provided for Native Americans. |
| **Step Two:** | Identify key historical events that led to decreased economic opportunity and access for Native American communities. |
| **Step Three:** | Reflect and journal about the key events you selected and the ways systems (policies and practices) have impacted present day realities. |
| **Step Four:** | Reflect and journal about the key events you selected and the ways systems (policies and practices) have impacted present day realities. |

The chutes and ladders of life unfold differently depending on a person's intersectional identities. Everyone may get to the finish line, but some members of society have to work harder, smarter, or take longer to get there, due to the impacts of oppressive policies and practices. Those who still achieve success, despite encountering a system of barriers, demonstrate strength, fortitude, and resilience in the face of less than favorable odds. It is vital to understand the contextual realities of privilege, oppression, and power, and how they systematically privilege certain identities over others (See Table 4.3: Historical Timeline Activity).

## CHAPTER CONCLUSION

This chapter explores both theoretical underpinnings and practical applications of systems understanding, a complex and challenging facet of cultural competence that we argue is integral and beneficial to engaging with others in diverse contexts. Learning exercises explored intersectional identities, sociological mindfulness, and historical context as crucial for knowing a group people and their positionality in history. Self-understanding about how our identities provide access and exclusion, opportunity and denial of opportunity in various life spheres, like community and business contexts and at work, can be revealing. Additionally, imagining what it would be like if our identities would shift paves the way for empathetic insight into how intersections of identity work in combination to privilege and/or oppress individuals and groups in various contexts. The second learning exercises focused on sociological mindfulness shows that seemingly harmless comments or jokes might be connected to broader social and cultural norms that reinforce power differences and also can be connected to institutionalized discriminatory practices. Everyday speech acts can reify power hierarchies. Finally, the final learning exercise in this chapter explores Native American history as a case study that reminds of the necessity to pay attention to the whole story, rather than simply judging or acting from a place of limited contextual understanding. In other words, we should all question what we are taught in mainstream society and seek multiple perspectives about the history, context, and cultures of groups of people we interact with. Legacies of privilege, rooted in history and context, contribute to present day inequalities and inequities. In essence, systems understanding is seeing, feeling, and understanding the big picture as it relates to the everyday parts that comprise the whole. Exploring the parts, the connections, and the whole is vital to systems understanding:

> Ultimately—as quantum physics showed so dramatically—there are no parts at all. What we call a part is merely a pattern in an inseparable web of relationships. Therefore the shift from the parts to the whole can also be seen as a shift from objects to relationships. (Capra, 1996, p. 37)

## REFERENCES

Arnold, R. D., & Wade, J. P. (2015). A definition of systems thinking: A systems approach. *Procedia Computer Science, 44*(2015), 669–678. Retrieved from: https://doi.org/10.1016/j.procs.2015.03.050

Banks, J. A. (2001). *Cultural diversity and education: Foundations, curriculum, and teaching* (4th ed.). Boston, MA. Allyn and Bacon.

Bello, B. G., & Mancini, L. (2016). Talking about intersectionality: Interview with Kimberlé W. Crenshaw. *Sociologia del Dirittom, 2*, 11–21. Retrieved from: https://doi.org/10.3280/sd2016-002002

Brantmeier, E. J. (2013). Toward a critical peace education for sustainability. *Journal of peace education, 10*(3), 242–258. https://doi.org/10.1080/17400201.2013.862920

Brantmeier, E. J., Aragon, A., & Yoder, B. (2009). Multicultural peace education: Empowering pre-service teachers toward a paradigm of social justice beyond color-blindness. In E. Ndura-Quédraogo & R. Amster (Eds.), *Building cultures of peace: Transdisciplinary voices of hope and action* (pp. 8–29). Cambridge, UK: Cambridge University Press.

Capra, F. (1996) *The web of life: A new scientific understanding of living things*. New York, NY: Anchor Books.

Collins, P. H. (2000). *Black feminist thought knowledge, consciousness, and the politics of empowerment*. New York, NY: Routledge.

Gardner, H. (2006). *Five minds for the future*. Boston, MA: Harvard Business Review Press.

Howard, G. R. (2006). *We can't teach what we don't know: White teachers, multiracial schools*. New York, NY: Teachers College Press.

Indian Health Service. (2019, October). *Indian health disparities*. U.S. Department of Health and Human Services. Retrieved from: https://www.ihs.gov/sites/newsroom/themes/responsive2017/display_objects/documents/factsheets/Disparities.pdf

King, M. L. Jr. (1967, December) *Interconnected World* [Sermon audio recording] Speakola. Retrieved from: https://speakola.com/ideas/martin-luther-king-jr-interconnected-world-massey-5-1967

Miller, J. P., Nigh, K., Binder, M. J., Novak, B., & Crowell, S. (Eds.). (2019). *International handbook of holistic education*. London, UK: Routledge.

Nhât Hạnh, T. (2009). *Interbeing: Fourteen guidelines for engaged Buddhism*. Full Circle.

Schwalbe, M. (2005). *The sociologically examined life: Pieces of the conversation*. Oxford, UK: Oxford University Press.

Sidanius, J., & Pratto, F. (1993). The inevitability of oppression and the dynamics of dominance. In P. M. Sniderman, P. E. Tetlock, & E. G. Carmines (Eds.), *Prejudice, politics, and the American dilemma*. (pp. 173–211). Stanford, CA: Stanford University Press.

Sidanius, J., Pratto, F., Van Laar, C., & Levin, S. (2004). Social dominance theory: Its agenda and method. *Political Psychology, 25*(6), 845–880. Retrieved from: https://doi.org/10.1111/j.1467-9221.2004.00401.x

Spradley, J. P. (1997). Ethnography and culture. In J. P. Spradley & D. W. McCurdy (Eds.), *Conformity and conflict: Readings in cultural anthropology* (9th ed., pp. 18–25). Boston, MA: Longman.

Spring, J. H. (2010). *Deculturalization and the struggle for equality a brief history of the education of dominated cultures in the United States* (6th ed., paperback). New York, NY: McGraw Hill.

U.S. Census Bureau. (2017, October 6) *American Indian and Alaska Native Heritage Month: November 2017.* U.S. Department of Commerce. https://www.census.gov/newsroom/facts-for-features/2017/aian–month.htm

Wilkins, D. E., & Stark, H. K. (2011). *American Indian politics and the American political system.* Rauman & Littlefield.

# CHAPTER 5

---

# S.O.S.

## Life-Long Path of Culturally Competent Engagement

---

We find after years of struggle that we do not take a trip; a trip takes us.
—*John Steinbeck (1962)*

To be in touch with the mind means to be aware of the processes of our inner life—feelings, perceptions, mental formations—and also to rediscover our true mind, which is the wellspring of understanding and compassion. (Nhât Hạnh, 2009, p. 3).

## CHAPTER OVERVIEW

Why walk the life-long path of culturally competent engagement in a deeper, contemplative way? Culturally competent engagement is about lifelong learning for the purpose of deeper connection and for the purpose of cultivating quality relationships with those who are culturally different from you. Seeing difference as an asset rather than a deficit affords us opportunities for positive relationships and potential social change. For those of us in helping professions or positions where we work with historically marginalized individuals and groups of people, we can more effectively position ourselves to help others from a place of authentic and empathetic understanding about their lived realities once we have cultivated

---

the capacity to see more deeply and understand one another more authentically. On this path, we cultivate the capacity to be aware of the body, the emotions, and the patterns of thought that can act as hindrances to our own growth and connection to other people. We can also interrogate structures and systems of oppression. When we begin seeing the complexity of people embedded in broader systems, we can more deeply see the *why* of certain conditions, behaviors, or responses of others. The hope is that this integrated and holistic perception can provide viable, proactive solutions to the complex challenges people face on a day-to-day basis in multicultural contexts.

In addition, effectively helping others from an understanding that our liberation is mutually dependent is insightful. A quote by Lilla Watson, a deceased Australian Aboriginal community educator and advocate, holds powerful instructive value for culturally competent engagement, "If you have come to help, you are wasting your time. If you have come because your liberation is bound in mine, then let us walk together." When approaching new multicultural contexts, understanding how power operates, checking one's assumptions at the door, and engaging with mindful humility and a stance of appreciative inquiry opens the possibility for mutual and shared understanding to emerge. With humility and a sense of not-knowing, a foundation for reciprocity is possibility, though considerable power dynamics need be navigated. Shifting power dynamics from power over/power up/power down approaches to power-with and power-within approaches holds promise for growth and change (Brantmeier, 2013).

Additionally, and simply stated, it is also enjoyable and fun to learn about what other people do, feel, value, and habitually think. Learning about oneself and others can be a fascinating journey, fueled by curiosity, and peppered with meaningful insight. For example, recall a moment when you took pause to grasp, truly grasp, a position on an issue (e.g., climate change, religious conviction, gun laws, or sexual attraction) that was profoundly different from your own. Did deeply understanding the perspective enrich your own life? The vast differences in cultural diversity provides needed variety, which some consider to be the spice of a vibrant life. Cultural differences are not to be changed, assimilated, or absorbed; rather, they are to be deeply understood, added to the tapestry of human experience, and celebrated. Culturally competent engagement, as a lifelong path or journey, can be an ongoing discovery of the mystery of the vast diversity of human cognition, group behavior, and collective emotion. Culturally competent engagement allows one to connect with others and validate who they are. Working with culturally and linguistically diverse populations can lead to connection, insight, and change. Change can be fear-filled but also exciting, and sometimes it is as easy as leaning into fear and choosing excitement.

Culture is a tricky bit—constantly informing thought, action, value, and meaning. We reproduce and co-produce the cultures that we inhabit and it is a shifting landscape—meaning that, just like nature, what appears to be constant has an undergirding rhythm of change that changes the present and the future. River water carves and responds to the rocks, and fallen tree branches. In the cycle of seasons, it rises and also becomes almost unseen and dormant. The river is not an entity unto itself, it is constantly influenced by all the elements, coming together and moving apart at great speed. Culture, in a highly connected modern world, is like the river; we are shaped and reinforced by a diverse array of streams, of influences—from social media, to our close personal relationships, to abrupt encounters with the other, to economic systems that circumscribe our choices as consumers. We find ourselves profoundly connected in a web of relationships, and we need only follow one line of connection to see how everything relates to each other; many rivers, one ocean.

In the Self-Other-Systems Model of culturally competent engagement that we wrote about in this book, the parts are related to the whole, the whole to the parts; you, cultural others, and the cultural systems we navigate and inhabit on a daily basis are interconnected. We are the same in some regards, and we are different in some regards. Honoring our similarities and accepting our deep differences is a profound act in culturally competent engagement. A mindful approach to culturally competent engagement is one that embraces a holistic approach to the self, other, and systems. Mindful thinking, feeling, and acting amid institutions and broader society are required. When we approach the world from a systems perspective, we experience relationships, not as objects, and from that connectivity, compassion, deep relationship, and love can flow. The following and final learning exercise for this book focuses on relationships and connecting with the self, with others, and with the systems that integrate our lives (See Figure 5.1: Self-Other-Systems Connections Diagram).

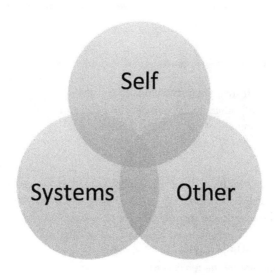

FIGURE 5.1.   Self-Other-Systems Connections Diagram

## LEARNING EXERCISE ELEVEN:
## SELF, OTHER, SYSTEMS INTEGRATION

*Overview*

With an attitude of humility and with a deep respect for the unknown, the cross-cultural sojourner moves forward, with cultural humility, to discover where their story lines converge and diverge in rather different directions. Learning to appreciate profound and deep difference is a life lesson. Pursuit of the question "Who am I" is a time-honored investigation in multiple wisdom-based, cultural traditions from around the world. In pursuit of self-understanding, one might ask "Who am I?" In pursuit of other-understanding, one might ask, "Who are you?" In pursuit of systems-understanding, one might ask "What causes and conditions created this "I" and "you"? The stories, that comprise our lives, have depth and nuance, and can be influenced by the smallest of incidents and insights. For instance, the right teacher or opportunity, at the right time in our life, sometimes appears and it is because of this chance, serendipitous, or random encounter that we pause, change course, or remain steady on the path.

In all honesty, we (Noorie and Eddie) cannot teach the golden recipes for culturally competent engagement; to the best of our knowledge, they do not exist. Each of us needs to honor our own journey, to find our way in community with others. We merely can provide tools for the path of exploring interconnectedness and deep diversity; we invite you to use the tools in this book to explore yourself, others, and systems. The following meditation aims to cultivate and integrate self, other, and systems awareness. You can either read it or download an audio recording from the Information Age Publishing website (Brantmeier, 2020).

*Learning Goals:*

Learners will make progress toward:

- Cultivate self-awareness and empathy for others;
- Integrate self, other, and systems awareness; and
- Share learning about mutuality and connection.

*Instructions*

- First, find a relatively quiet place to go inward and to focus.
- Close your eyes, or find an open, expansive, comfortable gaze on the floor. Be sure to take in the entire field of vision with eyes closed or open.
- The invitation here is to attune to your bodily posture. Align the spine in an upward fashion and feel the weight of gravity pulling your body toward the earth. Notice the tension of a gentle upward pull and a gentle sinking downward, and its effects on your body.

- Pay attention to the shoulders and gently roll them back, if necessary. This increases lung capacity and oxygen flow. Gently tuck the chin to increase communication between the brain and the rest of the body.
- Take a few deep, calming breaths and let wandering thoughts slowly become still. Be here now, in this precious moment.
- Focus on the breath as it enters the tip of the nostrils. In through the nose, out through the mouth. Breathing, simply breathing.
- Allow yourself the opportunity to be fully in this moment. Breathing, simply breathing. Open your mind and heart to what will come, trusting in the process.
- I will read a quote from Martin Luther King Jr. several times. The invitation here is to ponder the deeper meaning of the quote. Now, I will read the quote several times, emphasizing different words, in order for you to explore the meaning for you behind the words:
  - We are caught in an inescapable network of mutuality, tied in a single garment of destiny. Whatever affects one directly, affects all indirectly (King Jr., 1967).
- What message do you think is the quote trying to transmit? What do you learn about self, others, systems?
- (Repeat several times, allowing minutes of silence between repetitions.)
- Now, I will read a quote by Lilla Watson, an Australian Aboriginal educator and activist. The invitation here is to ponder the deeper meaning of the quote. Now, I will read the quote several times, emphasizing different words, in order for you to explore the meaning for you behind the words
  - If you have come to help, you are wasting your time. If you have come because your liberation is bound in mine, then let us walk together (Watson, n.d.)
  - (Repeat several times, allowing minutes of silence between repetitions.)
- What message do you think is the quote trying to transmit? What do you learn about self, others, systems?
- Sit quietly for a few minutes, experiencing this state of awareness, this state of contemplation.
- Prepare to open your eyes by moving the hands, and then the feet. Open your eyes slowly, gazing downward for three mindful seconds prior to engaging with ordinary, everyday awareness.
- If you did this meditation in a group, reflect with others about what you learned. If you completed this meditation along, do some mindful journaling about your thoughts and insights.

## Reflections

Both quotes used in this learning exercise hold layers of meaning and insight into connection and interdependence. The quote by Martin Luther King Jr. conveys how a common human destiny is apparent amid seemingly separate events

TABLE 5.1.   Self-Other-Systems Integration. Self-Other-Systems Integration

| | |
|---|---|
| **Purpose: Promote self, other, and systems understanding.** | |
| **Step One:** | Find a quiet place and tune into the body and emotions. |
| **Step Two:** | Simply breathe. |
| **Step Three:** | Deeply ponder the meaning of the Martin Luther King Jr. and Lilla Watson quotes regarding mutuality and connectedness of self and other. |
| **Step Four:** | Reflect about patience, acceptance, compassion, and advocacy. |
| **Step Five:** | Share what you learned with a friend or write about it via mindful journaling. |

and circumstances. In essence, what impacts one group either positively or negatively in society, has a ripple effect on the whole of humanity. If oppression exists for some individuals and groups, the oppressors are also negatively impacted, even if they are not aware of how they are negatively impacted. The Brazilian scholar and activist Paulo Freire, in the book *Pedagogy of the Oppressed*, explains something similar when describing how both the oppressed and the oppressor are de-humanized in the context of oppression. Re-humanization would require challenging the oppressive structures and systems that perpetuate dominant and subordinate relationships. Re-humanization would require a new way of being and relating to one other; a new way being and relatedness rooted in the insight and practice of mutuality and connection conveyed in the Martin Luther King Jr. quote in this the learning exercise.

In her quote, Lilla Watson conveys a warning and an invitation, simultaneously, for culturally competent engagement. With a helping mentality, one approaches other from a position of power and sympathy, a place of feeling sorry for someone else and their conditions. This approach, though well intentioned, can be quite harmful to communities. It positions the well-intentioned helper as a "savior" of sorts and can reinforce division and harm. Rather, Lilla Watson invites others into a relationship of mutuality, one of trust, of common struggle, of common hope and change, as we walk together toward an uncertain future. However, before we walk together, one must recognize how our own destiny is bound in a mutuality with all people, especially those who are different from you and who have different life circumstances. Systemically, we need to understand the causes and conditions that create injustice, inequality, inequities, and we need to work together to disrupt, dismantle, transform, recreate, and envision a more just and peaceful world (See Table 5.1: Self-Other-Systems Integration).

## CHAPTER AND BOOK CONCLUSION

The ideas expressed in this book are fundamentally simple, yet the path to embody and live the ideas can be long, demanding, and exciting. We hope the ideas and learning exercises presented will encourage you on your path toward mindful, culturally competent engagement. We are in it together, with all of our deep differences and profoundly connective human similarities. If we focus on our common-alities too much, we deny how the daily realities of difference oppress, repress, and deny access, opportunity, inclusion, and hope. If we focus on differences too much, we lose sight of our connectedness and common human-planetary destiny. Interdependence and differentiation are the poles of mindful cultural competence.

You will benefit tremendously as a person from exploring yourself, cultural upbringing, and patterned ways of thinking, feeling, and acting in the world. You will be enriched beyond measure from practicing other-centeredness and from appreciating profound differences. Diversity multiplies and fuels possibility and innovation. Our recommendation is to find a middle path, an understanding of tension and harmony amid diversity and unity. The deeper we reflect on how our destinies, both human and the natural world, are tied together, the more skillful our responses can be to pressing global issue such as: poverty; division; conflicts and war; climate change; food and water scarcity; and other wicked problems. How will we face the conflicts of the present and the future? If we face them with narrow self-interest and a protective, scarcity-oriented mindset, trouble awaits for all. Realities of climate change, dislocation, famine, and resource scarcity are inevitable. How individuals, groups, and societies respond to these pressing chal-lenges matters. We can become part of the solution with intention and informed action.

What if we faced the challenges of our time with mindfulness, connection, compassion, and hopeful action? Our actions and commitments to culturally com-petent engagement can build bridges and create a little more peace and justice in a too-often violent world, for ourselves and for the children of the world. Build-ing bridges, an often-used metaphor, is useful because a bridge connects separate land masses and allows travel over otherwise impassable bodies of water or rough terrain. Bridges connect and unite. Is it not our duty as global citizens to become self-aware, to hone our skills of connection with others, and to develop the com-plex thinking capacities necessarily to understand this interdependent world? Is it not our duty to connect and unite? As a mindful and active citizen, we all need to do our part to build bridges across difference, and to question and change unjust structures and systems.

We hope for a sustainable world for our children, similar to what our parents, grandparents, and ancestors hoped for us. Our human ancestors exhibited noble resiliency amid the slings and arrows of time. And here we are—a powerful spe-cies on this planet. Yet with power comes tremendous responsibility and the need for humility. We hope for a sustainable world for all planetary occupants. Let us be mindful of our consumption, tend to our connections, and disrupt systems that unjustly divide—together. Culturally competent engagement is a life-long path that can lead to meaningful and illuminating connections; it also will help us see the beauty and profound necessity of diversity.

## REFERENCES:

Brantmeier, E. J. (2013). Toward a critical peace education for sustainability. *Journal of Peace Education, 10*(3), 242–258. Retrieved from: https://doi.org/10.1080/174002 01.2013.862920

Brantmeier, E. J. (2020). *Learning exercise self-other-systems integration final.* Retrieved June 25, 2020 from: https://www.infoagepub.com/products/culturally-competent-engagement

King, M. L., Jr. (1967, December). *Interconnected world* [Sermon audio recording] Speakola. Retrieved from: https://speakola.com/ideas/martin-luther-king-jr-interconnected-world-massey-5-1967

Nhât Hạnh, T. (2009). *Interbeing: Fourteen guidelines for engaged Buddhism.* Full Circle.

Steinbeck, J. (1962). *Travels with Charley: In search of America.* New York, NY: Viking.

Watson, L. (n.d.). *About. Lilla.* International Women's Network. Retrieved from: https://lillanetwork.wordpress.com/about/

# ABOUT THE AUTHORS

**Dr. Edward J. Brantmeier** is a Professor in the Learning, Technology, and Leadership Education Department and Assistant Director (Scholarship Programs) of the Center for Faculty Innovation at James Madison University, U.S.A. In 2009, Ed was a Fulbright-Nehru scholar who lectured about multicultural peace education peace at the Malaviya Centre for Peace Research at Banaras Hindu University in India, as well as several other institutions of higher education in India and Nepal. He has guest lectured for the Center for Justice and Peacebuilding, Eastern Mennonite University (USA) and for the UNESCO master's program in Peace Studies at the University of Innsbruck, Austria. At James Madison University (USA), he teaches courses on sustainable peace leadership, cross-cultural education, and foundations of American education. He is integrally involved in diversity, inclusion, and equity initiatives across the university. He also consults with organizations on topics related to diversity, equity, inclusion and on increasing cultural competence via contemplative practices.

In terms of scholarship, Ed has published over 35 articles/book chapters, including five co-edited books: *Transforming Education for Peace* (2008); *147 Practical Tips for Teaching Peace and Reconciliation* (2009); *Spirituality, Religion, and Peace Education* (2010); *Re-envisioning Higher Education: Embodied Pathways to Wisdom and Social Transformation* (2013); and *Pedagogy of Vulnerability* (2020). Additionally, Ed co-edited a special edition of the *Journal of Peace Education* that focused on critical peace education (2011). He served as a founding co-editor of a book series on peace education (14 volumes) with Information

*Culturally Competent Engagement: A Mindful Approach,* pages 91–92.
Copyright © 2020 by Information Age Publishing
**91**

Age Publishing (2006–16). He serves on the editorial board of the international *Journal of Peace Education* and *Infactis Pax: Journal of Peace Education and Social Justice*. Ed has been invited to present his research on peace education, and related topics, in England, Cyprus, India, Nepal, Brazil, Germany, and widely in the United States.

**Dr. Noorie Brantmeier** is an Associate Professor in the Learning, Technology and Leadership Education Department at James Madison University. She also directs the graduate program in Adult Education/Human Resource Development. Noorie teaches graduate research methodology and diversity courses in addition to an undergraduate senior capstone. She has previously taught Ethnic Studies and Native American Studies at two other institutions. Her scholarship interests include measuring attitudinal change in diversity courses, HRD student competency development, the scholarship of teaching and learning, community development with Native American communities, and using technology to enhance research methods.

Noorie is also a founding partner of Seven Sisters Community Development Group, LLC a women and 50% Native owned consulting firm. As a consultant she focuses on strengthening organizational self-sufficiency, team building, leadership, and using data to strengthen organizational performance in mostly rural and Native American communities. She also facilitates diversity dialogues and consults on curriculum revisions integrating diverse voices and perspectives. Noorie received her bachelor's degree from Indiana University-Bloomington, her Master of Social Work from Washington University in St. Louis where she studied as a Kathryn M. Buder Scholar in American Indian Studies and is currently a Faculty Affiliate there, and her Ph.D. from Colorado State University.

CPSIA information can be obtained
at www.ICGtesting.com
Printed in the USA
LVHW082339160920
666291LV00011B/1801